Robot Framework Test Automation

Create test suites and automated acceptance tests from scratch

Sumit Bisht

BIRMINGHAM - MUMBAI

Robot Framework Test Automation

Copyright © 2013 Packt Publishing

First published: October 2013

Production Reference: 1181013

Published by Packt Publishing Ltd.
Livery Place
35 Livery Street
Birmingham B3 2PB, UK.

ISBN 978-1-78328-303-3

www.packtpub.com

Cover Image by Vivek Sinha (vs@viveksinha.com)

Credits

Author
Sumit Bisht

Reviewers
Syed Mohd Mohsin Akhtar
Ismo Aro

Acquisition Editor
Pramila Balan

Commissioning Editor
Mohammed Fahad

Technical Editors
Dipika Gaonkar
Mrunmayee Patil
Sonali Vernekar

Project Coordinator
Michelle Quadros

Proofreader
Stephen Copestake

Indexer
Rekha Nair

Graphics
Abhinash Sahu

Production Coordinator
Melwyn D'sa

Cover Work
Melwyn D'sa

About the Author

Sumit Bisht currently works as a Senior Software Engineer at a software service outsourcing firm. He has experience in both project and product-based companies and has done Masters in Computer Applications in addition to self-taught learning as part of his learning process towards making computers work. He has keen interests in leveraging various open source technologies for developing better software, considers himself a polyglot programmer and has experience working with different programming. While not working, he devotes his time in learning new researches and technologies, reviewing technical books on a wide variety of topics, sharing interesting information, and evangelizing open source philosophy through his blog, sumitbisht.blogspot.in.

I'd like to thank Vikram Mohan Sujanani for introducing me to the Robot Framework, while being my patient mentor, and Jayanti Kumar Srivastava for his support and expertise while unraveling elements of the framework. The entire Packt Publication team has worked tirelessly and persistently towards making this book a reality, and deserve a pat on the back. I am also grateful to Syed Mohd Mohsin Akhtar for reviewing this book. Last but not least, a huge thanks to Pekka Klärck and other members of the open source community for making available this versatile software and painstakingly extending help to various users.

About the Reviewers

Syed Mohd Mohsin Akhtar is a Software Engineer (R&D) at Encardio-Rite Electronics Pvt. Ltd., Lucknow, India. He received his M.C.A.(Hons.) from GBTU, India and eventually earned his spot as Software Engineer at DataBorough India a research subsidiary of DataBorough UK. He also has a specialized degree in Computer Maintenance from Aligarh Muslim University, India. He has been a Microsoft Student Partner, member OSUM (Open Source University Meetup), and an active member within several technical forums in his college days. He loves to work as a hobbyist in the areas of Computer Science and electronics. He can be contacted at mohsin.bcm.amu@gmail.com.

> First of all, I am grateful to Almighty "Allah" for giving me strength.
>
> I would like to express my sincere gratitude to Packt Publishing, for giving me the opportunity to have a first look at the book, and Sumit Bisht the author of this book for recommending me to review his book.
>
> At last I would like to thank my parents, family, and my friends.

Ismo has a long history of working in agile projects as a change agent. He has a strong focus in modernizing ways of working and quality of work. Quality assurance is close to his heart and he has worked as a Product Owner of the Robot Framework, leading the development of it, and implemented good testing practices company-wide.

At the moment he is working for Basware Corporation as a Lead QA Engineer, responsible for bringing in world-class Agile Testing and Test Automation. His previous employers have been Nokia Networks, Nokia Siemens Networks, and Ericsson.

> I want to thank my lovely wife and my two amazing kids. You are always in my heart.

www.PacktPub.com

Support files, eBooks, discount offers, and more

You might want to visit www.PacktPub.com for support files and downloads related to your book.

Did you know that Packt offers eBook versions of every book published, with PDF and ePub files available? You can upgrade to the eBook version at www.PacktPub.com and as a print book customer, you are entitled to a discount on the eBook copy. Get in touch with us at service@packtpub.com for more details.

At www.PacktPub.com, you can also read a collection of free technical articles, sign up for a range of free newsletters, and receive exclusive discounts and offers on Packt books and eBooks.

http://PacktLib.PacktPub.com

Do you need instant solutions to your IT questions? PacktLib is Packt's online digital book library. Here, you can access, read, and search across Packt's entire library of books.

Why Subscribe?

- Fully searchable across every book published by Packt
- Copy and paste, print, and bookmark content
- On-demand and accessible via web browsers

Free Access for Packt account holders

If you have an account with Packt at www.PacktPub.com, you can use this to access PacktLib today and view nine entirely free books. Simply use your login credentials for immediate access.

Table of Contents

Preface

Testing is essential for any activity to succeed; this applies to software as well. It not only covers verification but also the validation of the software. Commonly used testing practices include unit and functional testing that validates the needed functionality. However, manual efforts by testers or stakeholders are required to verify that the software being tested works as desired, as part of the software acceptance process.

As software has grown both in size and amount over the years, the acceptance testing process has become automated, leaving behind vast information in the form of audit trails of tests that need to be made available to the user at a glance and without which the purpose of acceptance test automation is defeated.

The Robot framework provides this missing link that integrates with the testing tool used for performing acceptance testing over the software or the "system under test" and structures this execution into discrete structures of tests arranged in a proper hierarchical manner; this not only results in execution in the desired manner, but also generates orderly reports.

Being an open source framework, this tool does not limit you to simply performing acceptance testing in a hierarchical manner and generating automated reports, but also allows you to customize it and create your own tool or even use it with other tools as part of a custom test environment setup required for your team.

What this book covers

Chapter 1, Getting Started with the Robot Framework, explains the need for acceptance test driven development, offers a high-level overview, and gives different methods of installation of the Robot Framework tool. It also discusses the various commands available for the user to interact with the framework and demonstrates simple test project creation and execution to the user.

Chapter 2, Configuring a Test Project, explains the test hierarchies and covers the different files and tables used in the framework as well as different syntax options to write the test files. It explains the commonly used test practices and explains how information can be re-used within the tests.

Chapter 3, Further Test Customization, covers test re-use, connectivity to external data sources and test templates, and user-defined keywords. It also provides different test writing styles and offers comparison with some other famous behavior-driven test tools.

Chapter 4, Extending the Framework, demonstrates real-world testing challenges and offers practical ways of using various built-in and external libraries to solve these challenges. It covers both the Web-based and desktop testing through object-oriented as well as image-based tests. In the absence of a compatible testing library, it also demonstrates the creation and integration of a custom written library.

Chapter 5, Generating Reports, covers the generated output of the tool in detail and offers different ways to customize the reports as well as the logs generated through the built-in as well as custom mechanisms. It also encourages the user to leverage the source code to create a customized reporting mechanism in the existing framework.

What you need for this book

In order to use the Robot Framework, you first need to install Python (the examples have been tested against 2.7, but you are free to use any version between Python 2.7 or 3), which might be installed if you are using a popular Linux distro or Mac OS X as your OS. Apart from Python, you can also install Jython and IronPython that can be used to run Python-based applications and tools such as the Robot Framework on JDK or .NET Framework runtime. A few examples do require explicit use of Jython, but the rest of the available environments can be used with any Python-based runtime. To install third party tools, or for easier installation, it is recommended to use easy_install Python module. Installations for tools/frameworks needed alongside testing with the Robot Framework are provided where necessary.

Who this book is for

As this book is focused on a testing tool, it primarily targets the testers. However, given the necessities of creating an in-house flexible testing tool, a hands-on Python development is also needed to modify and develop a testing framework to suit one's needs. Similar to DevOps movement, developers today are seeking ways to look beyond test and behavior-driven development, and the testers are also required to be more productive through means of automation. In this book, you will have to wear both the developer's and tester's hat in various situations in order to gain knowledge of this tool's working from both the perspectives.

Conventions

In this book, you will find a number of styles of text that distinguish between different kinds of information. Here are some examples of these styles, and an explanation of their meaning.

Code words in text are shown as follows: "We can include other contexts through the use of the `include` directive."

A block of code is set as follows:

```
# This code block runs 5 times for values of x between 11 and 15
|   | :FOR | ${x} | IN RANGE | 11 | 16 |
# This code block runs 5 times for x = 10, 12, 14, 16,18
|   | :FOR | ${x} | IN RANGE | 10 | 20 | 2 |
|   |      | Log  | ${x} |
```

When we wish to draw your attention to a particular part of a code block, the relevant lines or items are set in bold:

```
'<div id="top-right-header">' +
  '<div id="report-or-log-link"><a href="#"></a></div>' +
  '<div id="my_custom_image"><img src="../Pictures/github-
  icon.jpg" /></div>'+
  '</div>', {
generated: window.output.generatedTimestamp,
```

Any command-line input or output is written as follows:

```
pybot --randomize tests all_tests
```

New terms and **important** words are shown in bold. Words that you see on the screen, in menus or dialog boxes for example, appear in the text like this: "On specifying the **Fail** option, the user is further requested for the failure message before failing the test."

Warnings or important notes appear in a box like this.

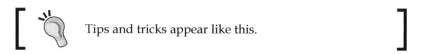

Tips and tricks appear like this.

Reader feedback

Feedback from our readers is always welcome. Let us know what you think about this book—what you liked or may have disliked. Reader feedback is important for us to develop titles that you really get the most out of.

To send us general feedback, simply send an e-mail to feedback@packtpub.com, and mention the book title through the subject of your message.

If there is a topic that you have expertise in and you are interested in either writing or contributing to a book, see our author guide on www.packtpub.com/authors.

Customer support

Now that you are the proud owner of a Packt book, we have a number of things to help you to get the most from your purchase.

Downloading the example code

You can download the example code files for all Packt books you have purchased from your account at http://www.packtpub.com. If you purchased this book elsewhere, you can visit http://www.packtpub.com/support and register to have the files e-mailed directly to you.

The code files for all the chapters are also present on Github at http://github.com/SumitBisht/RobotFrameworkTestAutomation which you can download, fork, and modify as you like and send any suggestions or corrections there as well.

Errata

Although we have taken every care to ensure the accuracy of our content, mistakes do happen. If you find a mistake in one of our books—maybe a mistake in the text or the code—we would be grateful if you would report this to us. By doing so, you can save other readers from frustration and help us improve subsequent versions of this book. If you find any errata, please report them by visiting http://www.packtpub.com/support, selecting your book, clicking on the **errata submission form** link, and entering the details of your errata. Once your errata are verified, your submission will be accepted and the errata will be uploaded to our website, or added to any list of existing errata, under the Errata section of that title.

Piracy

Piracy of copyright material on the Internet is an ongoing problem across all media. At Packt, we take the protection of our copyright and licenses very seriously. If you come across any illegal copies of our works, in any form, on the Internet, please provide us with the location address or website name immediately so that we can pursue a remedy.

Please contact us at `copyright@packtpub.com` with a link to the suspected pirated material.

We appreciate your help in protecting our authors, and our ability to bring you valuable content.

Questions

You can contact us at `questions@packtpub.com` if you are having a problem with any aspect of the book, and we will do our best to address it.

1

Getting Started with the Robot Framework

In this chapter we will cover the following topics:

- Definition and need for acceptance testing
- Introduction and a brief history of the Robot Framework
- Components of the Robot Framework
- Various installation methods
- Different installation environments
- Creation and execution of a sample project
- Brief description of the generated files

This book introduces you to the Robot Framework, which is a Python-based, keyword-driven, and acceptance test automation framework. It is very flexible and easy to use and extend according to your intentions. Built to provide acceptance test regardless of the platform size and scope of the software to be tested, also known as System Under Test (SUT), it is an ideal software tool to structure and manage different tests as part of a comprehensive test suite. Since this tool utilizes and manages the tests as well as deals with the software under test, it is beneficial for both testers and developers alike. Today, with the rise of versatile software tools and greater emphasis on test-driven development, the line between tester and developer has become blurred. To learn and use this tool effectively, you will have to put yourself in the shoes of both tester as well as a developer. The Python and/or ports into Java and .Net framework such as, Jython and Ironpython are also required.

As with any other physical creation, software is built with an aim of directly or indirectly changing our lives to solve a task or desire of someone. However, programming is an abstract science that is not dependent upon its end-user's desires, commonly referred to as garbage in – garbage out. A difference between the created software and its expected behavior by its user determines its implementation by the user. Thus, the end user must accept the software that is intended to be sold to him. However, the user often does not wants to be involved in the finer details and just needs to get the things done as he envisages with each iteration of the software. In order to perform this, the interactions that the end user does with the software is needed to be verified beforehand, which has led to creation of testing especially designed to perform this process of testing and verification. This process is known as acceptance testing. However, as the software grows, more and more, acceptance tests come up that give rise to a sense of chaos as upon failure of a test, proper context is not easily identified.

As the scale and complexity of software has grown up, so has the need for its quality assurance. Manual tests often are quite easy to set up, but they give diminishing returns of scale and are only feasible up to an extent, where a tester can manually work through different scenarios and identify bugs and errors in time without affecting the delivery schedule of the resultant product.

The need for acceptance testing

For tests that are large in size or complexity, a structured approach can help you to pinpoint the errors, which arise while testing for the system is carried out under test's acceptance. Increase in the development speed and efficiency as well as create accountability for various features of the software are also taken into consideration. These benefits can be summarized as follows:

- Pinpoint application failure
- Reduced error rate
- Provide automation and reusability
- Create a test audit trail

Pinpoint application failure

Through testing, it is possible for you to identify complete or partial failures as well as identify bottlenecks in performance that might have slipped during development or in other forms of testing.

Reducing the error rate

Through automation, the predetermined steps involved to run the program can be performed exactly as desired with no interference as well as no extra or erroneous user interactions. This is different from monkey testing as in acceptance testing; only the happy path scenario is to be dealt with.

Providing automation and re-use

Testers or any other human resources are expensive than computation cycles. So it is best to automate the repetitive tasks, which will also reduce time that is normally spent in typing, clicking, and digesting the user interface as well by the test user. Furthermore, test can be reused or iterated over, which reduces the amount of tests while making sure that the complete acceptance testing remains while you can focus on other problems.

Creating the a test audit trail

By keeping a record of various test results, you can gather interesting facts about acceptance testing such as how much of the system under test is covered under acceptance tests as well as how many failures were reported. This can be useful in changing management as well as re-engineering/modernization of the existing software.

What is the Robot Framework?

The Robot Framework is an open source, general purpose test automation framework used for acceptance testing and streamlines it into mainstream development, giving rise to the concept of **acceptance test driven development (ATDD)**. While commercial and in-house automated testing tools have been used traditionally to provide this kind of test automation. It suffers from the problem of reinventing the wheel and vendor lock-in as well as lack of flexibility to use tests with different software and under different circumstances. It stands out from other tools used for the same purpose by working on easy-to-use tabular test files that provide different approaches towards test creation. As different projects require acceptance testing in various ways, there is a need to make tests flexible, as the Robot Framework is flexible and extensible enough for handling these scenarios.

It is the extensible nature of the tool that makes it so versatile that it can be adjusted into different scenarios and used with different software backend. While it is most popularly used with selenium as a website automation tool, it can also be used with image-based testing software like **sikuli** and also with software that require remote access over multiple machines while only running the tests over a given machine. All of these can be made easily available through creation of custom libraries, which link up the Robot Framework configuration code keywords with tasks associated with whatever software the Robot Framework is using. On the other hand, the output that the framework produces can also be used in multiple ways, first of which is the HTML report and log file that not only produces a XUnit styled output, but also contains test operations in detail while signifying the execution order and test hierarchy of entire tests. This contrasts with the optional .xml generation that can be useful in further manipulation of the processes. One such example is creation of customized programs that use the information obtained by running tests to create a wide variety of results. Another example is the log files' subsequent use in continuous delivery environments that can allow a build to continue or fail based on all the individual acceptance tests which are in use.

It was created by *Pekka Klärck* as part of his master's thesis (http://eliga.fi/Thesis-Pekka-Laukkanen.pdf) and was developed within Nokia Siemens Networks in 2005. Its second version has been open sourced under Apache License, Version 2 since 2008 and has an active community of volunteers. It is available at http://code.google.com/p/robotframework.

The Robot Framework ecosystem

The following diagram presents a conceptual, high-level overview of the framework, and offers an insight into various components involved:

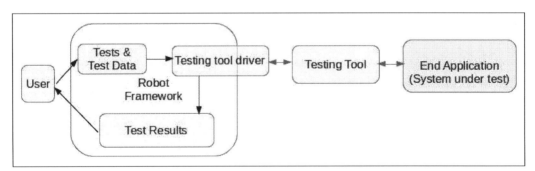

This can be explained broadly as follows:

- **Tests & Test Data**: This is the configuration of the tests, the closest to what most testers of the framework will be. It comprises test and data files and folders as well as the contents of those which dictate the test execution.
- **Test Results**: These are the end products of the tests, which are used to determine the results of tests as well as logs that can be used to assess various portions of the test.
- **Robot Framework**: This is the core framework that performs the actual heavy lifting to get things done.
- **Test tool driver**: This provides communication between the framework and the actual tools in place. It can be custom-tailored to meet specific requirements by the testing tool in place.
- **Testing Tool**: This is the actual software that is used to perform acceptance testing.
- **End Application (System under test)**: This is the actual software that is to be tested for usability for its acceptance by the client or the end user.

Installing and setting up the Robot Framework

The current version of the Robot Framework requires Python 2.7 for setup.

As of now, only pybot script gets created from a Python environment. In case of other environments, only the corresponding execution script gets created. If you happen to have multiple environments, then installation of different scripts is also possible. This differs from the previous versions where on installation, both pybot and jybot scripts were installed.

For custom installation, you will require Python, Jython, or Ironpython pre-installed; and environment PATH variable set correctly as the Robot Framework will use the first Python binary available on PATH or the exact library if supplied with the python command. You can verify this from the command line:

```
sumit@darkstar066:~$ python --version
Python 2.7.4
sumit@darkstar066:~$ jython --version
Jython 2.5.2
sumit@darkstar066:~$
```

On the project downloads page, there are various options, listed here under the following self-explanatory headings.

Source installation

To use the source, you can either download the zip containing sources or clone the project using mercurial hg clone: `https://code.google.com/p/robotframework`.

This will clone the project in the current directory and then you can either straightaway install the project, or make some modifications for customizing the framework.

Now go to the folder where source is checked out/unzipped and perform the following commands based upon the environment present:

```
python setup.py install
```

The preceding command installs the Python based version with pybot and rebot runner scripts.

```
jython setup.py install
```

The preceding command installs the Jython based version, with jybot and jyrebot scripts.

```
ipy setup.py install
```

The preceding command installs the Ironpython based runtime with ipybot and ipyrebot scripts.

If you see this folder, along with standard `setup.py`, there is another file, `install.py`, that can be used to install (it is the similar as installation from `setup.py`), reinstall, or uninstall the framework that can be used as follows:

```
python install.py in      [Installation]
python install.py un      [Uninstallation]
python install.py re      [Re-Installation]
```

To install with Jython or IronPython, replace `python` with `jython` or `ipy` respectively in the command. You may have to use `sudo/run` console as administrator if you run into any authentication errors, depending upon the user privileges.

```
sumit@darkstar066:~/repo/robotframework$ ls
atest           INSTALL.txt  PACKAGING.txt  robot_postinstall.py  tools
build           LICENSE.txt  pom.xml        rundevel.sh           utest
COPYRIGHT.txt   MANIFEST.in  proto          setup.py
doc             nsn.png      README.txt     src
install.py      package.py   robot.bmp      templates
sumit@darkstar066:~/repo/robotframework$ python --version
Python 2.7.4
sumit@darkstar066:~/repo/robotframework$ sudo python setup.py install
running install
running build
running build_py
copying src/robot/utils/misc.py -> build/lib.linux-i686-2.7/robot/utils
running build_scripts
running install_lib
running install_scripts
changing mode of /usr/local/bin/rebot to 755
changing mode of /usr/local/bin/pybot to 755
running install_egg_info
Writing /usr/local/lib/python2.7/dist-packages/robotframework-trunk20130614.egg-info
sumit@darkstar066:~/repo/robotframework$ ▮
```

Installing from source with python

One-click graphical installer

If you happen to be running Windows XP (32-bit), than you will want to use the one-click installer that installs the Robot Framework as well as Python and optionally, Jython and sets the paths without requiring any intervention. Other graphical installers for windows also exist in 32 and 64 bit versions.

Java environment installation

You can use the standalone jar that contains a bundled Jython as well as the framework. You just need to have Java installed on your system to execute the runnable jar for its installation.

In this method, instead of a command, the jar file is executed:

```
java -jar robotframework.jar run [options] data_sources
```

The Python package installation

The pip install mechanism only requires, you to have the Python and package managers such as `easy_install` or `pip` installed on your computer. To install this, you just have to type `pip install robotframework` or `easy_install robotframework` from the command prompt and the Python based Robot Framework gets installed.

Note that, for Python to run correctly, you'll need `elementtree` module as the default one is already broken.

The user can install more than one environment simultaneously on a computer and use the specified commands separately without affecting either of the installations.

Support for different runtimes

The Robot Framework not only works on the native python (`CPython`/`pypy` installations), but also supports Java and .NET based runtimes in the form of Jython and ironpython respectively. While there are some features that are exclusive to native Python-or Jython-based Robot Framework installations, most of the functionality is equivalent on all the runtimes. As people might have different OS and application software a stack setup according to their needs or desires, so they can integrate this tool in their existing runtime without requiring a separate runtime.

Based upon the installer environment used, the Robot Framework will create appropriate startup and post-processing scripts:

Environment	Startup command	Post-processing command
Python	pybot	rebot
Jython	jybot	jyrebot
Iron Python	ipybot	ipyrebot

In addition to these commands used in starting the execution, the Robot Framework can directly be started through the `robot.run` module itself if the standard Robot Framework is installed. This can also be used instead of the standard commands as the commands also call the module internally. The module can be called if the Python command in use is the one that has the Robot Framework installed:

```
python -m robot.run
jython .../run.py
ipy -m robot.run
```

This is handy if the Robot Framework is called by some the Python script. Instead of executing the scripts separately, you can call the framework from inside the same program easily.

The post processing command is useful to recreate test executions in the long run. After the test has been executed, you can save the XML file generated as output without saving any other file. To recreate the report and log files again in future, the `robot` command can be used which takes the XML file as an argument and results in the generation of the log and report files without recalling or running the actual tests again.

Command details

The `Pybot` command provides the following major options:

Options	Description
-N --name <name>	Sets the name of topmost test suite in the test hierarchy — thereby effectively customizes those areas.
-D --doc <documentation>	Sets the documentation of the top level test suite.
-M --metadata [name:value]	Sets the metadata of the top level test suite.
-G --settag <tagname>	Sets the given tag to all executed test cases.
-t --test name	Selects the test cases available by performing a pattern match against them.
-s --suite name	Selects the specified test suite by its name and also allows for the test reports to have the desired name instead of the name picked up by file/folder name.
-i --include tag	Selects a test for execution on the basis of its tag name.
-e --exclude tag	Opposite of include tag.
-R --runfailed output	Selected failed tests of earlier test runs have another goal.
-c --critical tag	Tests having this tag are considered critical (default for all tests).
-n --noncritical tag	Tests having this tag are overridden to be of non-critical type.
-v --variable name:value	Set variables in tests, only scalar variables($\{\}) are supported.
-V --variablefile path	Specify explicitly the file that contains variables.
-d --output dir	Specify the desired directory where resultant files are placed.

Options	Description
`-o --output file`	The generated XML output file.
`-l --log file`	The generated HTML log file.
`-r --report file`	The generated HTML log file.
`-x --xunit file`	xUnit compatible result file (not created by default).
`-b --debugginge rake`	Debug file written during the execution(not created by default).
`-T --timestampoutputs`	Adds timestamp and provides a custom title to all output files.
`-L --Loglevel`	Threshold level for logging and logging and test order customization.
`-W --monitorwidth`	Specify the width of monitor output.
`-C --monitotcolors`	Specify whether to use color on console or not.
`-K --monitormarkers`	Specify test success on console for each test that passes.
`-P  --pythonpath path`	Additional locations to search test libraries from.
`-E -escape what`	Specify escape characters in console with common representation.
`-A --argumentfile path`	Specify a text file to read more arguments in tests.
`-h -? --help`	Prints detailed help for the command.
`--version`	Prints the version of the installed Robot Framework.

A small exercise

To demonstrate the Robot Framework, we will create a simple dummy application as follows:.

1. Create a folder named `simpleapp`, this will serve as the application root folder.

2. Inside this, create a folder named `testsuites`, this will contain all the test configuration files.

3. Within the `testsuites` folder create a file, `Test_Case_1.txt`, with the following contents:

   ```
   ***Test Cases***

   First Test Action  log  this is a basic test
   ```

Note that there are two spaces before and after the log keyword.

4. Now run the project by calling Pybot script and passing the testsuites folder as an argument. You should get something similar to the following screenshot:

```
sumit@darkstar066:~/simpleapp$ pybot testsuites/
==============================================================================
Testsuites
==============================================================================
Testsuites.Test Case 1
==============================================================================
First Test Action                                                  | PASS |
------------------------------------------------------------------------------
Testsuites.Test Case 1                                             | PASS |
1 critical test, 1 passed, 0 failed
1 test total, 1 passed, 0 failed
==============================================================================
Testsuites                                                         | PASS |
1 critical test, 1 passed, 0 failed
1 test total, 1 passed, 0 failed
==============================================================================
Output:  /home/sumit/simpleapp/output.xml
Log:     /home/sumit/simpleapp/log.html
Report:  /home/sumit/simpleapp/report.html
sumit@darkstar066:~/simpleapp$ █
```

This confirms that the project has run successfully. You can view the results and log from generated HTML pages and perform future calculations over the data by using the XML file.

As we used a simple log statement, you get a logged message in the out log, as shown in the following screenshot:

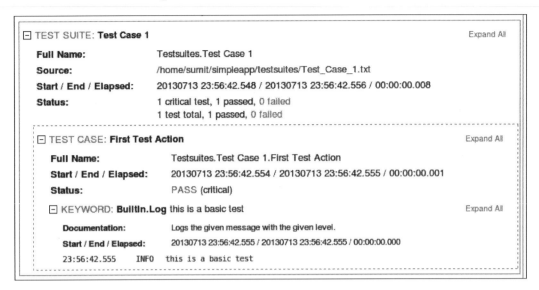

The generated XML is also easy-to-read (as shown in the following screenshot), which can then be used by any other external tool as an input parameter—thereby reducing the human intervention between different stages of testing if this process is also automated.

```xml
<robot generated="20130721 22:12:22.183" generator="Robot trunk 20130614
(Python 2.7.4 on linux2)">
 -<suite source="/home/sumit/testrf/testsuites" id="s1" name="Testsuites">
  -<suite source="/home/sumit/testrf/testsuites/1__first_test" id="s1-s1" name="First
   Test">
   -<suite source="/home/sumit/testrf/testsuites/1__first_test/1__Test_Case_1.txt"
    id="s1-s1-s1" name="Test Case 1">
    -<test id="s1-s1-s1-t1" name="Case present">
     -<kw type="kw" name="BuiltIn.Should Contain">
      -<doc>
        Fails if `item1` does not contain `item2` one or more times.
      </doc>
      -<arguments>
        <arg>Hello world</arg>
        <arg>world</arg>
      </arguments>
      <status status="PASS" endtime="20130721 22:12:22.238"
      starttime="20130721 22:12:22.237"/>
     </kw>
     <doc/>
     <tags> </tags>
     <status status="PASS" endtime="20130721 22:12:22.238" critical="yes"
```

Summary

In this chapter, we studied the need for acceptance test-driven development and how can we use the Robot Framework to achieve it. Various methods of installation were discussed over the supported platforms namely Python and its ported equivalents in form of Jython and Ironpython. We then proceed with exploring various commands that are available to perform various tasks as well as their possibilities. Later we created and run a basic test over the Robot Framework that validated the correctness of our setup. Lastly we examined the output files generated to get a look and feel of the framework.

Now that the basics have been covered, it is time for us to learn about the syntax, the different available actions, and different files involved in the Robot Framework project; which will enable us to write tests with various formats and be aware of the various options that are allowable in tests.

2
Configuring a Test Project

In this chapter, exclusive focus is on the structure and files contained in test. The topic has already been touched upon briefly in the first chapter, but a closer look at them would help set the background for further exploration as tests are the most important feature of the Robot Framework. The following major topics will be covered in this chapter:

- Creating a Robot Framework test file and a testsuite.

- Understanding differences in syntax across different file formats used in configuration. Gaining knowledge about the different configuration files.

- Understanding and utilizing setup and teardown operations

- Increasing automation through test re-use

We will start by explaining, what a test is and how it can be defined. Different type of tests and common naming conventions along with examples will be explained thereafter. Test file structure and their supported formats will be understood by the end of the chapter.

The Robot Framework makes it very easy to change the test configuration used in a project once the project has properly been set up. However, it is best to understand what tests really are, and how should they be organized before diving deep into specific implementation.

Similar to the development of conventional software, tests can either be created in top-down manner with the big picture upfront or a bottoms-up approach, where the tests are created first and integrated later.

In the Robot Framework, you are encouraged to follow the top-down approach where the test structure is created first, before creating and writing down the actual implementation. While this is not enforced, it is useful towards writing big and sustainable tests and is the recommended way of creating a test.

Tests are organized in a tree-style structure that consists of testsuite, testcase, and testaction. This convention has been followed in most of the structured testing and is a widely followed convention. A testsuite is a collection of different tests and other testsuites, and provides a logical unit for a set to perform tests. A testcase is a complete test for a particular task. A testaction is the smallest element in any test and is atomic in nature, which only validates a given condition.

Test naming conventions

Test naming conventions are important for the standardization and coherence of the tests. It also indicative of the quality of tests as the naming and placement of tests; and the use case scenarios indicate their order and relevance, which can be very useful when the tests are maintained in future.

Creating an execution order

In order to name tests, the Robot Framework is very peculiar; it uses the configuration file and folder names to determine the execution order and test naming.

For example, consider the following arrangement of different test files and folders in the test project in the file system:

```
application/

 tests/

  Test1.txt

  Other tests/

   Another test.txt
```

Running the pybot in the application folder will result in creation of different testsuites in the report based on the order of their presence in the file system. The following screenshot shows the file structure of a Robot Framework test:

```
|-- results
|    |-- log.html
|    |-- output.xml
|    `-- report.html
|-- run.bat
|-- run.sh
`-- testsuites
    |-- 1__first_test
    |    |-- 1__Test_Case_1.txt
    |    `-- 2__Test_Case_2.txt
    |-- 2__different_file_formats
    |    |-- 1__a_tsv_file_test.tsv
    |    |-- 2__a_tsv_file_test.txt
    |    |-- 3__pipe_separated_test.txt
    |    |-- 4__markup_formatted_test.html
    |    |-- 5__grid_table_formatted_test.txt
    |    |-- another_test.txt~
    |    `-- a_tsv_file_test.txt~
    `-- 3__an_empty_testsuite
```

After running, the tree command lists out the file/folder hierarchy. Here, the Robot Framework will infer the test hierarchy, group the tests, and nest test suites in form of files and folders. From this example, you can observe the following:

- The testsuites folder will be the root test suite.
- The folders such as 1__first_test beneath the testsuites folder will act as nested test suites.
- The test files contained within these folders will be the further nested test suites.

For example, tests contained in `testsuites/2__different_file_formats/2__a_tsv_file_test.txt` will be nested, which can better be explained from the following screenshot:

- Test suite hierarchy is detailed in the log file. In order to organize the results, it is important to ensure proper naming. So, instead of using spaces, underscore "_" should be used (as demonstrated in the preceding example).

- In order to get proper ordering irrespective of the test names, prefixing the test configuration with numbers can be done.

Test randomization

Sometimes, there may be requirement to explicitly disregard the execution order and run tests in random order. In that case, you can use the randomize option in the pybot command. This has the following options:

- To randomize all the test suites as well as the tests contained within them:

```
pybot --randomize All all_tests
```

- To randomize suites without affecting the tests contained within the lowest level suite:

```
pybot --randomize suites all_tests
```

- To randomize only the tests within the suites, the suite execution order is unchanged:

```
pybot --randomize tests all_tests
```

- To remove any randomization, if set in the command line:

```
pybot --randomize none all_tests
```

 The command arguments are read from left to right, and randomize option can come more than once.

In case of applying proper naming conventions like the following example, the example's test hierarchy will result in more understandable tests and the execution order of the tests can be easily predetermined. You can now easily infer the order of execution and hierarchy that will be present in the following order:

```
application/

  testsuites/

    1__Software_initialization.txt

    2__main_screen_checks.txt

    3__test_aux_controls/

      1__check_user_details.txt

      2__check_aux_control.txt

    4__check_values/

      1__primary_values.txt

      2__footer.txt

      3__links_to_other_controls.txt
```

. . . .

It is noteworthy that the only exception to this naming rule is in form of initialization files, which are named as __init__ followed by the extension as used in other test files. As there is only one init file per folder, it is clear that such a file contains information about its folder and the information contained in it pertains to the test suite itself.

Test file structure

So far, it has been demonstrated that whitespaces play an important role in configuration files. The test configuration is written in a tabular format with each column having separate elements such as test element. The Robot Framework allows flexibility in specifying the separations among the different columns in a test file as well as supporting different formats for the test files, which you can choose at your discretion. Note that depending upon the file extension; a suitable parser is selected during runtime. Some of the supported formats are as follows:

- HTML
- TSV
- Plaintext
- Piped text
- RestructuredText

HTML format

In an HTML format, the HTML is read, which comprises of different tables for different portions of the test configuration. For each table, the first heading element is read and based on this information; the rest of the table is understood. A word of caution! Any data that is outside the recognized table is discarded. You can understand this better with the help of following example:

```
<table>
  <th>Test Case</th>
  <th>Action</th>
  <th>Argument</th>
  <th>Argument</th>
  <tr>
    <td>First Test Action</td>
    <td>Log</td>
    <td>This is a test written in HTML</td>
  </tr>
</table>
```

Note that in the first column of table heading denotes the table name and it decides the subsequent execution of all elements contained in that table. This is followed by other headings that signify the position and order of other data. The rest of table contents populate the desired information in the specified order. Here, instead of delimiting the data by two spaces, it is present in different columns of the table. This method needs most overhead and verbose metadata, but the tests are very viewer-friendly and confusion of how much space to keep is also reduced as you can view these files easily in web browsers as well as edit in HTML editors.

TSV format

In the tab separated value format, one can specify the different columns by passing the values separated by single tabs. One of the astounding features of this format is that it can be opened in any spreadsheet application, which gives you and other users greater control over the test configuration files. If the text editor in use supports viewing of whitespace (spaces and tabs), then it is a good idea to enable it in order to keep the tab separated test without any errors, as users can invariably mix the two, causing the tests to malfunction. Another appropriate way to create and maintain these tests is to use the spreadsheet application alone, which will reduce the chances of corrupting the test. On a spreadsheet (as shown in the following screenshot), the test file is more natural and intuitive to use as the columns are properly differentiated. If you are having prior experience in developing spreadsheet solutions but are new to the Robot Framework, your learning curve is considerably reduced and you may feel at ease while writing and maintaining tests in spreadsheets, which can also be formatted for better visibility and ease of use.

	A	B	C	D
1	*Setting*	*Value*	*Value*	*Value*
2	Library	OperatingSystem		
3				
4	*Variable*	*Value*	*Value*	*Value*
5	@{MESSAGE}	Hello World!		
6				
7	*Test Case*	*Action*	*Value*	*Value*
8	the hulk Test	Log	This is a sample log from a tsv file	
9	another case	Log	${MESSAGE}	
10				

Plaintext format

If test configuration file display is not an issue, then plaintext file is the best option as it is most readable and contains much less metadata, which makes version control easier. This method is the most widely used in this framework. However, you have to take care to ensure that the elements are properly separated and the column elements are delimited by two whitespace characters. If the arguments used in tests are small and have limited columns, then this is the appropriate display format. The syntax and placement of the elements in this way first require some acclimatization, but it becomes easier to create and modify test cases in this format as you do not need anything apart from a text editor for creating and updating the tests. Since the whitespaces need to be at least two or more, there is no way that more than a single empty column can be left in place. This might not seem problematic, but is quite handy, especially in situations where there is a need to provide for explicit whitespace separation for more than a single column.

Pipe-separated format

Very closely resembling the previous format is the pipe separated format that uses pipe characters within the document to delimit the different columns. This is used where different lines contain varying number of arguments that are hard to spot. Consider the following snippet of a test:

```
A Custom test  [Documentation]  this test is done to ensure product
quality matches the requirements
    Log  Starting the product quality test
    Verify the initial condition exists  Should Be Equal  ${Product}
Drill Machine
```

The verbosity of the test, in this case, makes it harder to read and understand the test. Even worse, if someone is modifying it, he can introduce errors by accident. For instance, the documentation has been updated as follows:

```
A Custom test  [Documentation] The test ensures that product quality
matches federal requirements
```

If you observe the whitespace at the end of [Documentation], there is only a single space, which clubs both the Documentation keyword and its argument into one and the Robot Framework cannot understand this, causing it to fail.

In order to rectify in the same text file itself, the Robot Framework offers the flexibility to use a pipe symbol (|) instead of two spaces. Barring the first character of line, this symbol is surrounded by spaces on both sides, so the preceding test becomes:

```
| A Custom test | [Documentation] | this test is done to ensure
product quality matches the requirements |
|     | Log | Starting the product quality test |
|     | Verify the initial condition exists | Should Be Equal |
${Product} | Drill Machine
```

This is more readable as the columns are now separated by the pipe. Note that the ending pipe at third line is not present as placement of pipe at the end of last column at any line is optional. If required within any column as a normal text, the pipe can be escaped using the backspace character. The escape string being (\|). Another advantage that this format offers over the plaintext format is that multiple columns can explicitly be declared empty and the test can still run correctly. This coupled with specific placement of the text in exactly the desired columns leads to creation of tests having very specific structure. Pipelines are also required to nest test structure in the presence of loops within the tests, which is similar to the indentation found in Python programming but is impossible in the Robot Framework as more than two whitespaces do not constitute an empty column or an indent in the test code (more on this later while discussing iteration within tests).

Restructured text format

The **ReStructuredText (reST)** text format is familiar with any Python developer as it is used in Python documentation. It is a plaintext based markup that can easily be used to create highly formatted documents, tables, and so on using only a simple text file and a predefined set of markers. The advantage that it offers is very lesser metadata is used and the file contains majority of text that can easily be version controller, edited, differentiated, and well as searched. The rest mark-up offers advantages of both the HTML as well as plaintext file.

Similar to the HTML format, the test data is defined within tables and the Robot Framework looks up for the first element of the table to determine whether or not the table is a valid test table and, if this is correct, then its type is determined and the rest of the elements are processed accordingly. In this format, empty cells in the first column need to have a \ or a .. symbol.

```
======== =========== =========== ========= =======
 Test Case      Action                       Argument
Argument        Argument
======== =========== =========== ========= =======
Custom check   [Documentation]    custom checks
\                            Log                     Starting checks
```

```
     \
     \                          Another Test          Should Be Equal
     ${Existing}      15.45


     ========  ===========  ==========  =========  =======
```

As tools to process rest markup are part of the docutils project, you will need to have Python docutils module installed in the Python instance that is executing the tests. The Robot Framework internally converts the rest files into HTML documents and in case of problems with this format; other tools can be used to convert rest structured documents into HTML, which can be used to run the tests.

This is the flexibility of the Robot Framework, which allows you to have different file formats and structures. There is more to such flexibility in the style of writing tests, which will be covered in further chapters.

Test configuration files

As mentioned before, the tests are stored in files and are clubbed in folders that act as test suite for the files. A test file can contain different sections, which can optionally be moved into other files dedicated specifically towards the work of that particular section. Thus reducing the length and complexity of the actual test file, which is helpful if the test size is very large.

The test configuration files apart from the actual test files and folders are:

Suite initialization files

A folder in the Robot Framework denotes a test suite for all the files and subfolders contained in it. As there is no way to specify metadata of the test suite except for the folder name, there is a provision for special files that pertain to the folder in which they are placed. As with specifying a directory as a module in Python, initialization files have to be named as __init__ and their extension can be any valid extensions allowed by the Robot Framework. The format of these files is the same as test case files, but apart from few exceptions, the test case options are not allowed.

The configuration specified here overlaps with the allowable configuration in test case files as well in case of defining tags, setup, and teardown actions as well as test case timeouts. However, the changes overridden in these files are applicable to the entire test suite in which this initialization file exists.

One setting that deserves a considerable mention is the presence of suite `setup` and `teardown`. These only get executed once before and after the execution of all the tests present in the given test suite as well as in any sub-test suites as well. Also, if there are any sub test suites within the test suite, then the initialization files of these will be run likewise too. An example for this could be as follows:

```
| Setting | Value | Value |

| Documentation | suite init file |

| Suite Setup | Log | This is the setup method for the entire suite |

| Force Tags | example |

| Suite Teardown | Log | This suite has ended |
```

External variable files

These are the files that contain the variables used in the test cases. The main purpose of specifying the variables in an external file is to follow the **DRY (Don't Repeat Yourself)** principle to minimize duplication as well as make changes into the variables at a single place without changing the rest of the test. These files provide the variables that they create to other files that require variable information, which is different from the variable section of the test, or the variable table which is only applicable for the test case in which it is defined.

 Note that variable names are case-sensitive. In order to differentiate between variables and other keywords, keep in mind that generally the variables are kept in uppercase but there is no such rule.

The variables are defined as `${Variable Name}` for normal, single-valued variables and as `@{Variable Name}` for a variable containing a list of different values.

In a test configuration file, when only the variable table is specified, then the test file becomes a variable file and on its usage, only the table starting with variables will be considered.

Structure

A variable file can typically store a large amount and type of variables. For example a variable file can have the following structure that declares various types of variables:

```
*** Variables ***
${Weather}  London  Cloudy  25
${humidity}  75
${MARKS}  65.5
@{DAYS}  Monday  Wednesday  Friday  Sunday
```

Python/Java files containing variables

The variables can also be created in a Python or a Java file as in certain cases a Python or a Java class might need to save some dynamic data value at runtime, which can be passed to the tests in need. Only restrictive thing is that the python class name should be the same as its module and the Java class must not be in any kind of package. The easiest way to do this is to place the Python/ Java source in the same location as the test file itself (but is not recommended if you are having a separate application or a large number of tests/scripts). If you need to refer some value from external service or application, then the source file used can be referred to populate its variables which can be used in the tests.

For instance, a hash can be set/modified as variable in the Python file as:

```
person = { 'name' : 'John Doe','age' : '26', 'grade' : 'A', 'gpa' :
8.9 }
```

And in a Java file it can be modified as:

```
public String name = "Robot Framework";
```

Also, it can be used in the tests as:

```
*** Setting ***
Variables  python_file.py
Variables  JavaFile.java
....
*** Test Cases ***
...
  Log  For ${person['name']}, the grade obtained was
${person['grade']}
  Log  You are using ${name}
```

Just as with any other variable defined in the test itself the variables specified in these programs can be used.

In a similar manner, there is a provision for getting variables from a special function in the Python/Java code as `get_variables`/`getVariables`. The variables have to be prefixed with LIST keyword failing, which they will be assumed as scalars and can only have a single value.

 The variables as well as function setting these variable are visible to the Robot Framework tests if they have default or higher scope in the classes.

While the variable defined in Java is usable only with Jython runtime, one can use the Python file in any Robot Framework runtime, as all runtimes basically descend from Python.

To use the variables present in a resource file into a test case, variables keyword followed by the absolute or relative path to the variable file (the `.class` or `.py` as the case may be) can be given. And the variables defined in the variable file can be used as they were defined in the variables table within the file itself like the following:

```
*** Setting ***
Variables  path/to/variablefile.py
Variables path/to/java_file.class
```

Resource files

Resource files are necessity when there is need to save the variable data as well as higher level user keywords. The term user keyword will be explained in this book later on, but it is suffice to say that a user keyword is basically a keyword that is not present in any library but in the same file or an external resource file.

Structure

The resource file cannot have test cases. Apart from this, it is the same as the test case file. In the actual test case file, this file will have to be imported by the name of Resource under the settings table. After specifying the resource, the file path has to be submitted, which can be absolute or relative to the test case in question.

As mentioned, the resource files specify the variables and custom user keywords, so it contain the tables for the variable definition and keyword definition along with the settings table that can allow for import of some external library as the user keywords might be there to act as an alias for some external library. An example of resource file can be as follows:

```
*** Settings ***
Resource   Path/to/another_resource

*** Variable ***
${USER}   Test user

*** Keyword ***
Print welcome message for   [Arguments]   ${USER}
    Log   Welcome ${USER}!
```

The creation of keywords adds to the available syntax in the tests and inside the test file, this can easily be used.

```
*** Settings ***
Resource  path/to/resource_file.txt

*** Test Cases ***
Test user defined keyword loaded from resource file
   Print welcome message for  Mister President
```

Test setup and teardown

During testing, there is a need for performing certain tasks that have to be carried out at specific times during the execution of the tests. These operations are typically carried out before and after the tests. These are known as test setup and teardown (often known as pre-conditions and post-condition) and are present universally across different structured tests, such as unit, functional, and even acceptance testing.

A test setup occurs before the beginning of a test and a test teardown occurs after the execution of a test. It is worth mentioning that a test teardown runs after the test irrespective of whether it is a success or a failure. The only condition when it will not execute is the unconditional termination of the test, which occurs during a test error. These portions of test contain pre-conditions needed for tests such as opening of the web browser to a particular page, setting up a database connection and so on. And when the test gets completed, closing the opened connections, browsers, or resources and ensuring any further operation do not carry any repercussions of the actions undertaken during the tests.

Role of setup/teardown in automated testing are as follows:

- Setup Test Environment
- Create test environment
- Load initial test data
- Repeat for each test
    ○ Set up individual test requirements
    ○ Perform operations and assert conditions
    ○ Clean up resources used for test
- Summarize/save useful information
- Restore environment state to its initial condition
- Analysis of the test execution

The setup and teardown operations can be applied to both test as well as test suite level. It is not applicable within the tests. If there is a need to insert it between different statements in the tests, there are chances that the tests are not written correctly and the test structure needs to be relooked and refactored into smaller tests and parameterized according to the requirements pertain to stories for individual tests.

Being a robust framework in itself, the Robot Framework offers the capabilities of using these operations under both test suites as well as individual tests. For test suite, one can use the initialization file and for individual tests. The settings table in the test file itself can be utilized that can contain test setup and test teardown settings or even inside the test case itself in form of setup and teardown action. Using None after specifying a condition signifies that particular operation is not possible. A brief overview of some feature is provided as follows:

```
*** Settings ***
Test Setup  Open database connection
.....
*** Test Case ***
Some test case  [teardown]  Close connection

Case without teardown  [teardown]  NONE

Alternative names  [Precondition]  some conditions
    [Postcondition]  Cleanup this mess
```

The test setup and teardown thus offer a way for us to take the repetitive portions of tests at a single place and do not repeat same set of instructions all over the place, thus setting up scene for test automation and re-use through test parameterization.

Summary

In this chapter, various files involved in the Robot Framework test creation and configuration together with the test naming conventions for different components such as, test suite, test case, and test action were discussed and the execution order management was detailed. As the test file format is quite different from any other test, it was exhaustively discussed as well. The use of variables as well as extra files are also discussed as these promote test code re-use and separate the test contents. Finally, the test environment management through test setup and teardown was discussed, which is essential if the tests require any prior dependency.

This serves as the groundwork for further work over the framework and as the basic syntaxes mentioned here are covered, the test automation and re-use will be discussed in the next chapter that continues from the work that has been covered here in order to automate and re-use existing tests.

3
Further Test Customization

This chapter covers syntax and styles necessary to create reusable test components for automated tests. Apart from the Robot Framework centric tests, it also covers an introduction to behavior-driven development and covers the following major topics:

- Need for test re-use
- Internal and external re-use
- Feeding data into test scripts
- Higher order test re-use
- Different styles of writing tests

Automation and agile

The agile manifesto places tremendous importance on usable code over conventional documents. It encourages practices such as extreme programming, which is a type of agile software development practice that improves software quality and makes the software development more responsive to the ever changing customer requirements. Amongst other important tenets of this practice is the automated acceptance testing. An acceptance test is simply some code that can be run and captures at its heart some aspect of the functionality of the system. The idea is that both the developer and the stakeholder collaborate on writing this test together, to capture the requirements in the code, which when passed, forms some kind of seal of approval. These are distinct from unit and integration tests as they are largely written by the developer, and for the developer. They help them emerge, validate design, and protect against errors. Acceptance tests are written by the stakeholder and the developer, for the stakeholder and the developer. Agile methodology places importance over tests as tests themselves become specifications rather than business reports or documentation.

A commonly used expression is that the difference between unit tests and acceptance tests is that unit tests helps you build the thing right, whereas acceptance tests helps you build the right thing.

As mentioned before, the Robot Framework as an automated acceptance test-driven development tool provides various capabilities out of the box and allows the user with enough flexibility to go about with automation to ensure that the software in question can always have its basic functionality in place.

Before proceeding with writing down the tests, it is necessary to know how to implement a design that will help scale and maintain the tests for future requirements. Similar to the creation of any other software, the tests written in modular fashion enable re-use through selection of different test modules as required. This can better be explained by the following diagram:

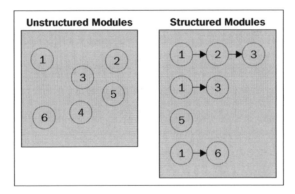

Here, it is evident that separation of test **1** into a unique module has enabled us to use the same set of tests in part of three other tests, thereby reducing the amount of repetition involved in writing if the tests were to be created manually.

However, generally, during acceptance tests, there are some portions that are unique to the situation under which the test is executing. Consider the following example that needs to perform acceptance testing for a large website consisting of hundreds of pages.

Test website module functionality:

1. Open the browser.
2. Go to the specific page URL.
3. Ensure that it is not an empty page/invalid URL.
4. Check whether the site headers and footers exist and are displayed properly.

5. Ascertain if the actual page content (excluding the header and footer) is not empty.

6. Search and verify whether a specific element exists in the page.

7. Close the browser.

Even in this brief test, there are innumerable possibilities and a single test cannot address all of them. For this reason, testers make copies of tests such as this and after making changes, put them elsewhere to meet another requirement. However, copying leads to presence of duplicate tests that are hard to change as change in the environment requires changes across the different tests. On the other hand, if there is test re-use, then changes in the re-used test at one place can reflect across different tests. To address the concern of uniqueness in different scenarios, one can parameterize the same test. In the preceding example, a possible parameterization can be as follows.

Test website module functionality(browser, URL, and content):

1. Open the **browser** (select the specified browser).

2. Go to the specific page **URL** (as specified in the parameters).

3. Ensure that it is not an empty page/invalid **URL**.

4. Check whether the site headers and footers exist and are displayed properly.

5. Ascertain if the actual page **content** (excluding the header and footer as specified in the parameter) is not empty.

6. Search and verify whether the parameterized **content** exists in the page.

7. Close the browser.

Now the same test can be used in a wide variety of scenarios (read pages) and different portions of the entire website can be tested for page contents using the same test.

As mentioned here, the same parameterized approach to create reusable tests can be applied to the Robot Framework through the use of variables. The variables can be used as an input mechanism from a given source of information which is not related with the test and the execution of tests occurs depending upon the obtained data. As repetition of test actions forms the cornerstone of test re-use, there is a possibility to repeat test actions even within the tests. While doing so, a single test or use case can repeat the same instructions again internally, often with some variable data that is unique to a specific repetition. These are detailed in the following sections.

Internal re-use

As mentioned earlier, repetition within the single test constitutes test re-use internally. Note that the data, if any, involved in different instances of the iterations might come from outside, but the repetition only occurs within the test action.

Loops and flow control

Having gained a good background of the syntax of writing a test, it is time to move on to the most common and convenient way of iteration, that is, a loop. Robot Framework solves this problem through the use of Python styled `for` loops, but that's easily understandable for the uninitiated as well.

It follows a straightforward syntax, the loop is started with FOR which is a special keyword. This is followed with a variable that is present within the loop. This variable is followed by a mandatory IN statement. This is followed by the variable or a collection over which the `for` loop is to run. Like Python loops, the subsequent statements are indented by a single space. As soon as the indentation stops, it is assumed that the body of the loop is finished.

All this seems like an iterative construct of any programming language, but in the Robot Framework there are a couple of exceptions, such as:

- The `for` loop can iterate with multiple variables
- The loop cannot have directly nested loops within itself, but can make use of custom keywords within the loops that can contain loops within themselves
- The **scalar variable** collection over which the loop iterates can be specified as different arguments

Note that the `for` loop requires explicit whitespace definition to clearly demarcate different columns as a simple text file with space/tab delimiters wouldn't do. If tried to run, it will print out the error message "FOR loop contains no keywords". This is because the body of the loop requires (an extra) indentation, which is not possible in simple whitespace as two or more than two spaces are only constructed as a single separation.

The `for` loop has a variant that allows for iteration over a range of values. This is idiomatic Python, but is quite convenient at times. Its syntax is: FOR keyword followed by a single variable. Next comes the In Range keyword that provides various range limits through arguments. This can be demonstrated as follows:

```
# This code block runs 5 times for values of x between 0 and 4
|   |  :FOR | ${x} | IN RANGE | 5
# This code block runs 5 times for values of x between 11 and 15
```

```
|   |   :FOR |  ${x} |  IN RANGE |  11 |  16 |
# This code block runs 5 times for x = 10, 12, 14, 16,18
|   |   :FOR |  ${x} |  IN RANGE |  10 |  20 |  2  |
|   |        |  Log  |  ${x} |
```

Flow control

At times during the loop iteration, there may be cases where the execution needs to be changed, which can be done either to skip the present and continue with the next iteration or to terminate the loop entirely.

Sometimes, the loop contents need to be processed in such a manner, which is not iterative in nature. In this case, we need to issue special commands that allow us to manipulate the contents of the flow of contents within the loop irrespective of the iteration status. In most conventional programming languages, this is specified by the continue and break constructs. Robot Framework offers a similar approach by providing some special keywords for this purpose in its default library.

Breaking off without finishing

By using the Exit For Loop or the Exit For Loop If built-in keywords, it is possible to terminate the loop and continue with the further statements:

```
|   |   |  Run Keyword If |  ${val} > 10 |  Exit For Loop
```

In the preceding example, Run Keyword if is used, which is present in the built-in library. As soon as its condition is evaluated to true, it is executed and the Exit for Loop keyword causes the loop to terminate. If the test case contains any other statements after the loop, then they will get executed normally.

This can be simplified through the use of Exit For Loop If keyword as it acts as a handler for the break operation without requiring a separate if condition and hence the preceding command can be rewritten as:

```
|   |   |  Exit For Loop If |  ${val} > 10 |
```

Continuing with the next iteration, similar to breaking the loop, sometimes there are exceptional cases where there is a need to continue with the next iteration of the loop before the present iteration has completed:

```
|   |   |  Continue Keyword If |  ${val} > 10 |  Exit For Loop
```

Note the use of the `If` suffix on various commands. The `If` statement is not a specific keyword, but many statements, such as the `Exit For Loop` and `continue` keywords, have alternate definitions that act conditionally in the presence of certain conditions.

Feeding external data

Tests can be fed data from any external data store such as a database, an Excel, or a CSV file or some external application that returns values dynamically and then can execute over the same data. To demonstrate this concept of test re-use further, we will undertake another exercise that focuses on performing the same task repeatedly. For the sake of the reader, we have abstracted the concepts now as these can then be implemented in whichever manner possible.

Basically, if we are having a set of repeatable tasks specified in a collection of values, then we can perform them in two different manners:

- Perform the set of tasks repeatedly inside a test for each value
- Perform the entire test repeatedly for the values

Performing a set of tasks repeatedly within a test

In this scenario, we create a test that takes in the argument or uses a variable containing a list of elements and iterate over it. As a precursor to this, first let us create the file containing the dynamic variable. Here, the system under test is a Python script that selects values out of current time in an array whose value we cannot predetermine:

```
import time
var = []
while(time.time()%10 <8):
  var.append(int(time.time()%10))
  time.sleep(1)
```

The preceding script first imports the `time` module as it will be used in the program later on. Next, the `var` array is created. This is followed by a `while` loop that checks the last decimal value of the currently elapsed time and checks if it is less than 8. If it is, then it adds this last value as an integer into the array and sleeps for a second to get another value. Although, the `var` array is not randomized, its size and contents are unknown beforehand, which makes the `var` array dynamic at runtime.

This lets us have the variable var with an unspecified amount of value. Now we can use it to better utilize collection of values within tests. Within the test, first this Python variable file is loaded and then the contents are iterated upon:

```
| *Setting* | *Value* |
| Variables | ./dynamic_variables.py |
| *Test Cases* | *Action* | *Argument* |
| List should exist | Variable Should Exist | @{var} |
| Variable not declared should not be there | Variable Should Not
Exist | ${val} |
| Iterate over Dynamic variables | :FOR | ${val} | IN | @{var} |
|                 |            | Log       | ${val} |
|                 | Log | finished iteration |
```

This will load the contents from the script, and iterate over the collection of values and perform a sample task over the value.

Application in test automation

The outlined concept of looping can be applied in test automation through the use of customized user keywords and loading of test data via an external program that can leverage any available data medium to load the data for the system under test. As explained earlier, this is useful in achieving test re-use and ensuring that as testers, we follow the principals of **Don't Repeat Yourself (DRY)**.

Higher order re-use

The tests can be repeated within the test suite through the creation and use of constructs of higher order that contain various test commands and at times even entire tests. This enables the tester to combine similar or equivalent user stories or use cases into a single test and provide different inputs depending upon the circumstances. Another significant advantage that test re-use offers is the overall clarity of the project. Tests if re-used have to be called from various places, thereby giving the benefits of DRY.

User keywords

As mentioned earlier, user keywords can be used to embed a part of test into a single custom keyword. These can be re-used and they can also specify arguments in their definition, which can be used to pass on test data parameters by the callers of these tests.

Test templates

Test templates are used to create components within a test that can accept different parameters at runtime. This is different from user keywords as the user keywords have to be called with their name and arguments by the caller, but templates are provided with only the data to be processed. A better picture can be obtained from a sample template that just logs the provided data to it:

```
Template to print params   [Template]   Log
                                         Alpha
                                         Beta
                                         Gamma
                                         Delta
```

This example provides the arguments to the template one at a time in order to get itself processed. Here the test repeats the operation specified by the templates to its arguments and the test effectively becomes the shorter version of the following actual test:

```
A normal test to print param
                    Log    Alpha
                    Log    Beta
                    Log    Gamma
                    Log    Delta
```

Note that this is a simple example of template that is only visible inside the test cases table. There are other possibilities in creation of a template that can be re-used across different tests. Through the use of templates, the test becomes more oriented towards data and the official Robot Framework documentation states that, through templates, the keyword driven tests can be converted into data driven tests.

User libraries

User libraries provide wrappers for implementing functionality into the Robot Framework. By using user libraries, we are able to extend the framework to provide for a certain task, or more importantly, extend the capability of this tool to work on some other tool. Conversely, to use a custom library, the Robot Framework test must follow the keywords made available by such a library and provide data to the necessary arguments, thereby fulfilling the keyword format contract that leads to correct execution of the tests. This technique of creating customized library and consuming it in various tests will be dealt in detail in the next chapter.

Approaches towards writing tests

There are various approaches involved in testing and it is often the different nature of various test writing styles that separates the tests from other forms of software development. Writing acceptance tests can either be done by using the standard and external library keywords directly as mentioned before, or by using some mechanism to simplify the text of tests and make them more readable from the perspective of a non-technical person. This is crucial in agile software development as the stakeholders are involved in the design of software early on that might not be technically inclined or requiring to understand the syntax of tests like a programmer. However, they can provide a vision of how an application is supposed to work or behave; their input and feedback are important.

The Robot Framework supports mainly three styles of writing tests. While the execution and output of the tests are not different, it is the nature of the test's syntax itself that separates it from a similar test written in a different style. These are explained in detail in the following section:

Keyboard-driven tests

Keyboard-driven test is the most commonly used technique where the test is broken down into different portions known as keywords, which determine the contents of the tests. These keywords may further contain other keywords or tests, which are able to be re-used and extracted wherever needed. Through the use of keywords, test constructs can be made abstract and multiple and/or complex statements can be added under a single keyword that can make the tests a lot easier to understand and its function can be easily understood.

To better understand this approach, consider the following test code, which uses the process library to open the Firefox browser with `google.com` as the opened page:

```
Start Process  firefox  google.com
```

Now consider the keyword approach:

```
Open google.com homepage in firefox browser
```

This does exactly the same as the previous code, but offers much clearer view in the test. Its implementation details can be hidden in the `Keyword` table as follows:

```
Open ${url} homepage on ${prog} browser  Start Process  ${prog}
${url}
```

Data-driven tests

The data-driven tests are useful while doing parameterization as the same test can be re-used with data comprising of different values. This makes tests like these versatile and without performing the same set of actions, one can easily have various test cases where the task to be carried out largely remains the same with only the inputs and outputs to be changed. This differs from the keyword-driven tests as these tests are coarser, granular, and depend on the test templates to provide the necessary tests in place as explained in the test template section earlier.

Behavior-driven tests

One of the popular styles that has recently seen an increased growth is the behavior-driven development. Creating tests that cover software behavior and writing actual software based on these tests is known as **Behavior-Driven Development (BDD)**. However, so far this book was dealing with keyword-driven acceptance test, which is quite rigid in its structure. To deal with automation, external data streams can be used and the tests can be fed this information based on the data. However, the tests can also be structured to suit the business user requirements oriented towards behavior. However, first we need to understand BDD before applying the same in our tests.

Behavior-driven development

Despite the obvious benefits of automated acceptance tests, in practice, even amongst experienced XP and TDD teams, it's rarely done, or done well. One of the reasons is that finding a stakeholder with the technical ability, interest, and patience to sit in front of a computer writing pure code for even a DSL like gerkin or RSpec is hard. Consider the following `rspec` test present in WEBrick (an HTTP server in Ruby commonly used in development):

```
should "be a WEBrick" do
  GET("/test")
  status.should.equal 200
  response["SERVER_SOFTWARE"].should =~ /WEBrick/
  response["HTTP_VERSION"].should.equal "HTTP/1.1"
  response["SERVER_PROTOCOL"].should.equal "HTTP/1.1"
  response["SERVER_PORT"].should.equal "9202"
  response["SERVER_NAME"].should.equal "127.0.0.1"
end
```

This example observes the behavior that is based on the response from the server, from this it can be concluded that the server is a WEBrick server or not.

However, at time this may be deeply integrated into the code of test and requires that the internals of the system under test are exposed to it. This is because the developer is required to provide the actual method calls/interfaces or code mocks or stubs of the software right into the `rspec` tests, which might be fine in projects involving developers, but is not feasible where black box testing, as in acceptance testing is required.

BDD using the Robot Framework

Robot Framework not only provides a DSL or a platform to easily write the code in a human-readable format, but also separates itself from understanding the internals of the concerned software as it only performs the acceptance testing for a given behavior. These tests only differ in the manner in which the user keywords take in arguments, which is done within the keywords themselves. Here these keywords comprise of multiple letters and describe a specific thing to do.

Standard libraries

The Robot Framework provides various keywords, which have been discussed so far. These are contained in the `builtIn` library and are available to any test by default. In addition to these, there are certain extra keywords that are part of the framework which are bundled as separate libraries and to use them, an explicit reference needs to be provided without any installation. These libraries are as follows:

- Collections
- Dialogs
- Operating System
- Process
- Screenshot
- String
- Telnet
- XML

Collections

This library uses the supplied lists and dictionaries from an external Python file and performs various operations, such as comparison and modification over it. Some keywords from the builtin library that operate over lists and dictionaries can also be used in conjunction with this library. For example, consider the following example where the Python file defines the following variables:

```
details = [1,'ssh', .034, 'main-repository']
user = {'name':'john doe', 'age': 21, 'account':'basic'}
```

These variables can be manipulated in the test as follows:

```
*** Setting ***

Library   Collections
Variables  filename.py

*** Test Cases ***

Lists   Should not be empty  ${details}
        Append to List  ${details}  12500
        ${custom}  Create List  1  ssh  .34  main-repository  12500
        Lists should be equal  ${details}  ${custom}

Dicts   Should not be empty  ${user}
        Dictionary should contain key  ${user}  name
        Dictionary should contain value  ${user}  21
        Dictionary should contain value  ${user}  basic
```

Similarly, other keywords belonging to the collections library can be used together with other libraries.

Dialogs

Dialogs provide a way to let the user input data during the test execution. Although this goes against the principles of automated testing, but is desired at times.

 Note that currently, this library does not work on IronPython runtime.

For instance, the following command lets the user pass or fail a given step:

```
Execute Manual Step   Perform manual operation and continue
```

This provides the following dialog box which waits for the user input to continue:

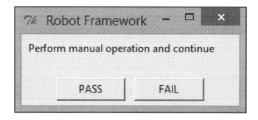

On specifying the **Fail** option, the user is further requested for the failure message before failing the test.

Similarly, the other keywords specified in this library can be used.

Operating System

This library provides the Robot Framework interaction with the OS environment, such as files and folders, environment variables, and the ability to call various processes. Most of the methods declared in this library are self-explanatory. However, keywords that manage processes are deprecated and are now also present in process library.

Process

This library allows the test to run external programs. It uses the sub process module in Python where the external process is spawned, the input/error/output message pipes are connected, and the return codes are obtained. It can either run process and wait for their termination or run the processes in the background. For better management, it can also terminate one or all the processes started by the test.

Screenshot

This library enables capture of screens during the Robot Framework test execution, which allows detailed reporting of the project if there are screens present in the test environment. If using with Python runtime, this will require additional libraries like wxPython or pygtk. Other runtimes provide an out of the box support for screen capture. The take screenshot takes the screenshot of the screen and saves it where the log file or the XML output is generated if no setting or file location is specified. If no name is given, then Screenshot_number.jpg is saved where the number gets incremented after every execution to create a unique saved image. Similarly, the width argument specifies how much area gets allocated to the image in the log file.

The following specifies the file name and size of screen capture image:

```
Take Screenshot    screenpic.jpg    width=500 px
```

This saves the following image and embeds it into the log file:

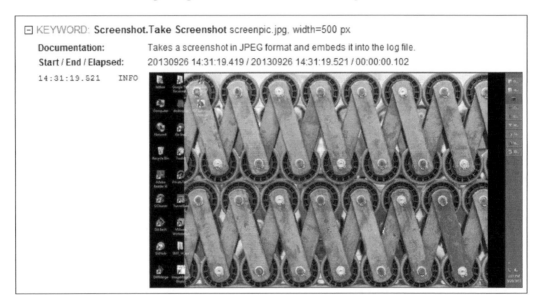

String

This provides the normal String operation, such as substring, replace, and splitting strings, as well as specialized functions that generate random string. This also contains utility methods that operate over strings present across multiple lines.

Telnet

This library enables the Robot Framework test to connect to a Telnet server and pass commands to run over the server. An easiest way to test this is to set up a test server on your machine itself. Considering you set the Telnet server correctly on your machine with user and password both set to `test`, then the following code will perform as desired:

```
*** Setting ***
Library   Telnet
*** Test Cases ***
Telnet Session   Close All Connections
    Open Connection   127.0.0.1   prompt=test
    Login   test   test   login_prompt=login:
      password_prompt=password:
    ${details}   Execute Command   ls-l
    Log   ${details}
```

Note that setting up prompt in the `Open Connection` command is not mandatory, but is needed for certain commands like the `execute` command. This library is sufficient for opening, closing, as well as changing between multiple Telnet connections and covers most of the Telnet features.

XML

This is the XML parser supplied by the framework and can be used to search and validate supplied XML file or text. It uses the ElementTree library internally and offers capabilities to parse and find different elements, attributes, values, and supports Xpath-styled lookup.

Remote test execution

The Robot Framework also supports the use of remote libraries, where a part of the test can be hosted as a server and can be used by other tests remotely. This is useful in centralizing a part of test at a single place and all the client tests can derive information based on that test itself.

It uses the XML-RPC protocol for the remote interaction and offers various capabilities for distributed testing, such as making different keywords available remotely that can be used to perform some operation over the remote server by different tests. Hence, a method in the remote library can be used to perform some task that can be called as a library keyword in the tests which provides re-usability of code across different tests.

To start off with the remote test, within the test, only the setting table needs to specify the location of the remote test:

```
Library   Remote   http://localhost:8567
```

On the server side, the following can be specified:

```
def strings_should_be_equal(self, str1, str2):
  print "Comparing '%s' to '%s'" % (str1, str2)
  if str1 != str2
    raise AssertionError("Given strings are not equal")
  else:
    return "Given Strings are not equal"
  if __name__ == '__main__':
    from robotremoteserver import RobotRemoteServer
    RobotRemoteServer(ExampleRemoteLibrary(), *sys.argv[1:])
```

Here, this file can be run from the Python command to set up a Robot Remote Server and the methods defined here can be used as keywords, such as `strings should be equal`. If you are wondering if the code needs anything more, then you need to download the provided `RobotRemoteServer` script file separately and place it besides this script. Currently, the servers for Python and Ruby are present, but other servers can also be created. Thus, writing distributed tests in the Robot Framework is trivial and can easily be used through HTTP.

Summary

This chapter dealt with the philosophy and style of writing the tests. As the tests should be written with automation in mind, both the internal and external re-use through iteration and parameterization of test cases as well as getting data into the tests was covered as these are amongst the important things to consider while going forward with the automation. Next, all three different writing styles consisting of keyword, data, and behavior driven tests was covered followed with brief discussion of importance of behavior-driven development and comparison with other development tools currently in popular use. This chapter provides all the remaining portions of the Robot Framework library and you can now confidently begin writing tests that can be automated and provide testing for small to large enterprise software systems by using the wide variety of tools and support provided within the framework itself. In order to extend the capabilities of the framework and make it usable with a wide variety of software, extensive focus will be made on user library in the following chapter.

4
Extending the Framework

This chapter is a bit different from all the previous chapters because it focuses on external libraries that provide interaction between the Robot Framework and the other software over which Robot Framework runs. This is important as the integration with other leading software is the cornerstone of this framework. Therefore, we need to be aware of the various libraries that are present as well as know how to create a custom library for the framework if there is not any.

Until now, all the examples have only used the `log` function present in the built-in library as this was the easiest way to demonstrate output on running the framework. While this was easy to understand, it didn't explain how acceptance testing is supposed to work in real world scenarios.

In this chapter, various third-party libraries are covered, which extend the Robot Framework in myriad ways. Briefly put, the following would be covered in this chapter:

- Web application testing through Selenium
- Debugging Selenium-based Robot Framework code through the REPL shell
- Testing Java-based desktop applications through the Swing library
- Introduction to image-based automation through Sikuli
- Creation of a custom Robot Framework library for Sikuli
- Overview of other libraries that assist in writing acceptance tests

To demonstrate the integration with a third-party library, we will finally proceed with using the Sikuli tool to capture and replay the mouse and keyboard actions, and using image-based computer vision to create a fully-fledged acceptance testing solution.

Testing the web applications

Today, most of the commonly used software in use are present on the Web as it has become the common medium to interact with huge amount of users worldwide. Creation of a web-based solution is not only getting easier by the day (as new technologies are coming up and the old ones are getting matured, optimized, and obsolete), but the connectivity, ease of use, and sophistication for web application clients are also increasing. Thus, the web applications which interact with the world today have almost negligible lead time between their development and end user interaction. Acceptance testing thus becomes essential as changes in the software must be validated quickly to ensure basic correctness and existence of basic functionality before they go live into the production.

Selenium

Selenium is a web browser automation tool that provides recording and playback facilities. It can be used to create simple scripts that can automate actions on browser and web pages by using various objects present in the browser. As it is a leading web browsing automation tool, there are various resources available for it. As a browser runner, various browsers have Selenium as a plugin/extension and can be installed within the browser itself. However, while running the custom examples, a Selenium-based server is required, which is present in an embedded JAR file that can be called directly. Originally, it came with a remote controller, which required a Selenium remote control server that managed browsers' web requests from the browsers. However, owing to the popular requests to simplify the development requirements, Selenium2 was created that used WebDriver to manage the browsers directly and perform operations, such as file upload and popup management directly from the browser. Through the use of WebDriver, the Selenium tests can be made more flexible and made to work in browsers that were not possible to be used by Selenium before.

The Robot Framework Selenium library

This library provides a bridge between the Robot Framework and the Selenium WebDriver engine. Through this, various Selenium commands can be issued directly from the Robot Framework test files. There exist separate libraries for Selenium1 as well as Selenium2 and depending upon the Selenium version, one can choose an appropriate library. There is no need to despair though, as Selenium2 library is largely built upon the contents of the Selenium library. One thing to be noted is that if Selenium is running with a separate server (an embedded Jetty server), then remote control driver is needed, otherwise the WebDriver can easily be chosen.

To install this library, `pip` can be used and depending upon the set up, sudo/admin privileges may be required:

```
pip install robotframework-selenium2library
```

The detailed documentation is present at `http://rtomac.github.io/ robotframework-selenium2library/doc/Selenium2Library.html`, which can be quite handy while developing these applications.

Running web-based tests

In the example, a small website has been created using flask, which is a Python-based micro framework to create dynamic websites. To run the example, flask would be required at the local Python setup, which can be installed as:

```
pip install flask
```

After installing flask, traverse to the `flaskApp` directory via command line and run the demo website by running its main controller file:

```
python hello.py
```

This starts up the flask on `localhost:5000`, and displays the following window:

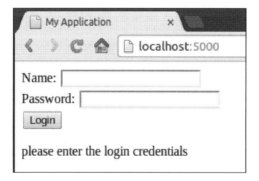

On entering wrong username/password an error is displayed on the same page. Here, the contents of the form are not persisted and only the presence of an error message indicates that a wrong username/password combination has been tried previously.

The following screenshot shows the error when a wrong username/password combination is tried:

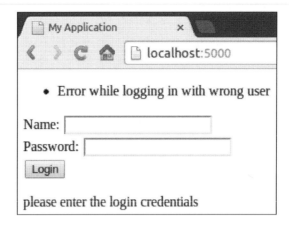

The application redirects to the respective page if the login is successful, which also provides a confirmation text mentioning the successful login as well as provides a URL for logging again, if there is any need to do that again, as shown in the following screenshot:

Using the Selenium2Library

To perform the same task through the Robot Framework, following test can be written with the help of robotframework-selenium2 library, which was discussed previously:

```
| Perform correct credentials | go to | ${LOGIN URL}
|   | Title Should Be | My Application
|   | Page Should Contain TextField | username
|   | Input Text | username | ${VALID USER}
|   | Input Password | password | ${VALID PASSWD}
|   | Click Button | Login
|   | Location Should be | ${SUCCESS URL}
```

This test assumes that the Selenium browser is already set up. There are a few variables in use that are quite obvious by their names. The test code is explained as follows:

1. On start of the test case, go to the specified URL.
2. Assert that the title of the page is `My Application`.
3. Assert that the page contains the desired elements.
4. Enter the valid user in the **Name** text field.
5. Enter the valid password in the **Password** text field.
6. Instruct Selenium to click on the **Submit** button, the browser then issues the form action.
7. As a result, the browser is redirected to another page, the URL of which is checked.

To see and run this full test, you are encouraged to check out the test code as well as view the Selenium library. Similarly, you can also assert contents in various pages for some specific text as a form of testing by using the `page should contain` keyword.

Debugging through the REPL shell

If you are starting with the Selenium library, you will face problems in setting up the entire Selenium setup. Thankfully, there is a tool that helps you run the test operations one at a time. This is known as the debug-library and is an REPL shell. **REPL (Read Evaluate Print Loop)** like any other console, only accepts a single line and presents its output before requiring the next line. This is quite similar to shells present in various other languages. Its source code is present at:

```
https://github.com/xyb/robotframework-debuglibrary
```

To install this on a machine running Python with its packaging manager, use the following:

```
pip install robotframework-debuglibrary
```

or:

```
easy_install robotframework-debuglibrary
```

After installing this, a command, `rfshell` is available. You can use it to perform basic operations and Selenium-specific tasks. The following screenshot shows an example:

```
● ● ●   sumit@darkstar066: ~
sumit@darkstar066:~$ rfshell
================================================================
robot debug b4Kxq
================================================================
REPL
>>>>> Enter interactive shell, only accepted plain text format keyword.
> help

Documented commands (type help <topic>):
========================================
EOF   exit   help   selenium

> help selenium
Start a selenium server, and open google.com or other url in browser.
>
```

As soon as `exit` is entered in the shell, it exits and a report HTML file is generated at the `home` folder of the user.

 Note that there is no log or XML file generated anywhere for this.

Testing desktop applications

Acceptance testing can also be implemented in desktop-based applications, making the Robot Framework tests far more applicable rather than just catering to the needs of some specific problem or a framework alone.

Testing through objects – Java Swing

Swing library is a fully featured library that can be used to test Java Swing-based applications. As this works on Java platform, this needs Jython runtime. To run an acceptance test over a swing application, two things are required in the `classpath`:

- Swing library JAR
- The actual swing application bundled as a JAR

On having the necessary files, the test can be used. The classpath can be set prior to the Jython command, or prefixed with the command itself like the following example:

```
CLASSPATH=swinglibrary-1.6.0.jar:myApp.jar jybot testsuites
```

Here, the `swinglibrary` is version 1.6.0 and the system under test is bundled as `myApp.jar`, and the Robot Framework files are present in the `testsuites` folder. The application is then visible to the Robot Framework test file and can be accessed through its fully packaged Java Swing name. The settings table of the test scripts will require the `swinglibrary` to be loaded in order to provide all the Swing library specific keywords.

A Swing test

Given the following application, the test will cover adding and deleting items to and from the given **Todo List**:

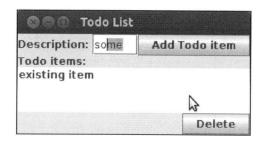

Just by looking at this Swing application, it is not distinguishable which text field, table, or any other UI element is talked about, so black box testing will not be successful in this case and we need some internals, such as various component names to interact with them. This might feel similar to Selenium as both the libraries provide object-based testing that requires knowledge of the internals of the system under test by the tests themselves.

Following is the test required to cover various use cases this UI has to offer:

```
| Start test | Start Application | fully qualified name of the
  application
|   | Select Window | Todo List
|   | Button Should Be Enabled | Add Todo item
|   | Type Into Text Field | description | Get this swing
  application tested.
|   | Push Button | Add Todo item
|   | ${itemCount}= | Get List Item Count | todolist
|   | Should Be Equal As Integers | 1 | ${itemCount}
```

This can be explained briefly as follows:

- Run the Java application through the `Start Application` keyword using the fully qualified name of the Java application (that is, the package and the class name) which is needed to run the application from the JAR file
- Select the correct window, which also ascertains that the application has the desired window
- Check for other basic assumptions, such as the state of various elements
- Perform various UI operations through intuitively named keywords for the same
- After typing text and clicking on the **Add Todo** button, the `todolist` size should increase

Similarly, other operations for the UI can be performed. Like other external libraries, it is helpful to have its library documentation by the side while writing tests in this library.

Testing through images

This section covers image-based testing, which is different from what has been covered so far. In image-based testing, the user interface is treated as a black box and no object internals of the applications are exposed.

Sikuli

Sikuli is a leading tool that performs automation through computer vision, that is, recognition of images on the screen. As a human being, we can distinguish an object's properties by looking at it, but this is not straightforward in case of computers as computers can only match binary or textual information. Thus, there is a need for computer vision or knowing if a given image is present on a larger screen or not. In simple sense, Sikuli uses the user-supplied screenshot images to perform action over various items and displays the generated script visually in the Sikuli IDE. Following is one such script to do a search:

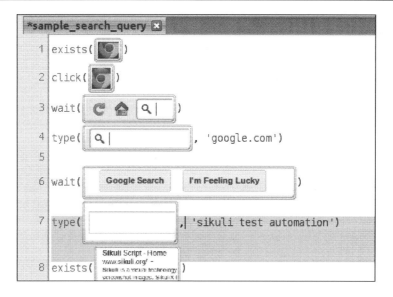

As is evident from the image, the script does the following:

- Check if the Chrome browser icon exists on the screen
- Click on the Chrome browser to open it
- Wait for the browser window to open up and display the URL
- Go to google.com in the URL bar, which will open up the Google home page
- Wait for the Google search buttons to show up
- Perform the desired query in the appropriate text field
- Verify the results obtained
- The Sikuli page should appear on the first page of results

However, behind the scenes, the following Python script is generated in the folder where this Sikuli script is saved:

```
exists("1377428833316.png")
click("1377428844996.png")
wait("1377428859228.png")
type("1377428922965.png", 'google.com')
wait("1377428949234.png")
type("1377429289183.png", 'sikuli test automation')
exists("1377429031446.png")
```

Apart from this Python script (or its HTML equivalent), there exist various images that are referenced in the test. The important thing is that at runtime, Sikuli runs computer vision software at its core that determines whether it gets a match for the image in the screen and acts accordingly. There is absolutely no need for having any knowledge of internals of the software under test. While this might seem counterintuitive at first, the lack of control over components and objects is compensated through image-based testing that liberates the test from the system under test, and the tests can thus operate over a wide variety of software platforms, from different desktop applications, mobile emulators, mainframe terminals, web-based, and remote applications using only the contents displayed on the screen as a basis for its input and decision making ability, just like a human being which is performing manual automated acceptance testing.

Creating a custom Sikuli library

Out of the box, the Robot Framework seems like a complex framework and creation of an external user library looks like a tedious task. However, there are times when requirements dictate the need of acceptance test solutions for this. Fortunately, open source solutions like Sikuli have an extensible application platform that is also very well documented. The custom integration of Sikuli with Robot Framework is created and demonstrated by *Mykhailo Moroz* (http://blog.mykhailo.com/2011/02/how-to-sikuli-and-robot-framework.html). The approach used in this method is discussed in the following section.

In order to use the Sikuli as a test validation engine, its API (http://doc.sikuli.org/javadoc) has to be exposed first, which can be done via a clever hack that uses the Python classes used internally in Sikuli. Since this will work in Jython environment, there is a need to have sikuli-script.jar in the classpath and create a wrapper around the Sikuli API in order to use various methods. The Sikuli API contains a Screen class that has various methods.

To make these methods present in the Screen class global, these methods are manually pushed into the internal global directory and are overridden by customized individual methods:

```
def sikuli_method(name, *args, **kwargs):

    return sys.modules['sikuli.Sikuli'].__dict__[name](*args,
    **kwargs)
```

This lookup is then used to pass the values from the customized methods into the native code that is present internally in the Sikuli engine. For instance, the `click` method can be implemented as follows:

```
def click(target, modifiers=0):

    try:

        return sikuli_method('click', target, modifiers)

    except FindFailed, e:

        raise e
```

This wrapper allows the creation of simple Python scripts that can run in Jython environment without requiring the Sikuli X test runner. As there is already `sikuli-script.jar` in the classpath, the tests so created can run without the Sikuli IDE, or in the headless mode.

As these scripts can run independently in the Jython environment, these can be run through Jybot that can employ various Robot Framework scripts that can call these script functions. This creates a solution to drive a collection of multiple Sikuli scripts as test cases in such an order that performs a large task through the collection of different small scripts.

To run this example, we need to have the following prerequisites:

- The Robot Framework installed correctly with the Jython runtime
- Sikuli is installed properly and `sikuli-home` environment variable points to its root folder

The following commands in the batch file runs the application by setting up the environment needed for all the softwares involved:

```
set sikuli_jar=%sikuli_home%sikuli-script.jar
set CLASSPATH=%sikuli_jar%
set JYTHONPATH=%sikuli_jar%/Lib
call jybot --pythonpath=TestLib ^
    --outputdir=results ^
    --loglevel=TRACE ^
    --output "%~d0%~p0results\output.xml" ^
    --log "%~d0%~p0results\log.html" ^
    --report "%~d0%~p0results\report.html" ^
    testsuite
```

Since, we are using different Sikuli scripts as different test cases, we will import these as custom tests in our Robot Framework test files, which are kept in the `testlib` folder in order to keep things simple in this example:

```
***Settings***
Library  TestAction1.XTest   WITH NAME   TestAction1
Library  2ndcase1staction.XTest   WITH NAME   2ndcase1staction
Library  anotheraction.XTest   WITH NAME   anotheraction
***Test Cases***
Test Case 1
  TestAction1.Execute
Test Case 2
  2ndcase1staction.Execute
  anotheraction.Execute
```

The `library` file is actually a customized Sikuli script written in Python that calls the Sikuli API to work as a headless Sikuli instance:

```
from __future__ import with_statement
from sikuliwrapper import *
addImagePath(common.cfgImageLibrary) #uses the values supplied by the
robot framework.
Settings.MinSimilarity = 0.9  # Image present on the screen should
match 90% or more than the provided image.

class XTest(BaseLogger):
    ROBOT_LIBRARY_SCOPE = 'TEST SUITE'

    def __init__(self):
        None
    def Execute(self, *args):
        type("this is a reference test example")
        wait(0.485)
        ...
```

To make these tests image-based, you can call functions such as `click`, `validate`, `type`, and so on, with the path to the sample image file used as its input argument.

Apart from the `test` and `library` files, there is a `sikuliwrapper.py` file, which provides Sikuli methods into these library file invocations:

```
from logger import *
from sikuli.Sikuli import Region as SikuliRegion
from sikuli.Sikuli import Screen as SikuliScreen
log = RobotLogger()
class VerifyException(RuntimeError):
```

```
        ROBOT_CONTINUE_ON_FAILURE = True
    # function for calling native sikuli methods
    def sikuli_method(name, *args, **kwargs):
        return sys.modules['sikuli.Sikuli'].__dict__[name](*args,
        **kwargs)

    # overwritten Screen.exists method
    def exists(target, timeout=0):
        addFoundImage(getFilename(target))
        return sikuli_method('exists', target, float(timeout))
    ...
```

Similarly, other Sikuli API calls can also be wrapped to provide an easy interface to the library file, which in turn is called by the Robot Framework test.

However, in case of image-based testing, failures should be descriptive. To do this, screenshot can be taken at the instance when something fails or succeeds, which requires you to create a custom logger:

```
import logging
import datetime
import shutil
from sikuli.Sikuli import *

# Properly set the logging mechanism
logging.addLevelName(logging.WARNING, 'WARN')
HTML = logging.INFO + 5
logging.addLevelName(HTML, 'HTML')

class RobotLogger(logging.Logger):
    def __init__(self, name='robot', level=logging.INFO):
        level = logging.DEBUG
        logging.Logger.__init__(self, name, level)
        self.addHandler(RobotHandler())

    def _get_unique_name(self, prefix="", suffix=""):
        now = datetime.datetime.now()
        return prefix + now.strftime('%Y-%m-%d_%H-%M-%S') + suffix

    def screenshot(self, msg='', folder='results/screenshots/',
    region=(0,0,1440,900)):
        name = self._get_unique_name(suffix=".png")
        img_src = capture(*region)    # Actual call to capture the
        entire screen
        shutil.copy(img_src, folder + name)
```

```
            self.html_img(msg, folder + name)

    def passed(self, msg, *args, **kwargs):
        self.info('PASS: ' + msg, *args, **kwargs)

    def failed(self, msg, *args, **kwargs):
        if self.isEnabledFor(logging.DEBUG):
            if len(getLastFoundImages()) != 0:
                self.html_img("Source Image",  'images/' +
                getLastFoundImage())
            self.screenshot()
        raise common.VerificationFailed(msg)

    def html(self, msg, *args, **kwargs):
        self.log(HTML, msg, *args, **kwargs)

    def html_img(self, msg, image):
        self.html('%s <img src="../%s" />' % (msg, image))
    ...
```

These are the essential files required to properly run and log the Sikuli-based applications easily with the Robot Framework. The output can be viewed in the following example by opening notepad and running the application:

```
>jybottest.bat
==============================================================================
Testsuite
==============================================================================
Testsuite.TestSuite1
==============================================================================
Test Case 1                                                          | PASS |
------------------------------------------------------------------------------
Test Case 2                                                          | PASS |
------------------------------------------------------------------------------
Testsuite.TestSuite1                                                 | PASS |
2 critical tests, 2 passed, 0 failed
2 tests total, 2 passed, 0 failed
==============================================================================
Testsuite                                                            | PASS |
2 critical tests, 2 passed, 0 failed
2 tests total, 2 passed, 0 failed
==============================================================================
Output:                                                              ence-test
-origin.
Log:                                                                 ence-test
-origin.
Report:                                                              ence-test
-origin.

C:\Docu                                                              -original
>
```

Untitled - Notepad

File Edit Format View Help

this is a reference test example
case changed
5 4 3 2 1 0

Other noteworthy libraries

There are various other libraries that extend the capabilities of the Robot Framework in areas that are not normally seen as candidates for acceptance tests, but will benefit from test automation, if done in the right way. Some of these libraries are as follows.

Testing network protocols

Rambock is a test library that provides an easy way to test various network packets, protocols, and message templates:

```
https://github.com/robotframework/Rammbock
```

It allows you to specify the custom protocol, its client and servers; messages, and both the traditional as well as custom protocols can be tested.

Testing the web services

Suds is a lightweight. but dynamic SOAP Python client for consuming web services:

```
https://github.com/ombre42/robotframework-sudslibrary
```

Testing the database

The database persistence and contents can be tested through the `robotframework-databaselibrary`. Here the database is queried to find out its state and perform things, such as running the SQL scripts:

```
http://franz-see.github.io/Robotframework-Database-Library
```

A similar library exists for interacting through JDBC, which is handy especially for databases that otherwise are not supported for testing:

```
https://github.com/ThomasJaspers/robotframework-dblibrary
```

Summary

In this chapter, a lot of external tools and libraries were discussed that extend the capabilities of the Robot Framework. First the web application testing was demonstrated through Selenium and its REPL shell that is handy to debug applications. Next, Java-based desktop application testing through the use of object-based testing was demonstrated. The Sikuli application and image-based testing was explained along with an in-depth case study which further explored the extensibility of its API to create a Robot Framework-friendly solution. Finally, some of the other popular libraries were listed.

In the next chapter, we will look into test reporting operations to understand what the different outputs generated and how can we perform various desired operations with generated reports and customize test outputs.

5
Generating Reports

While creating and executing tests does provide numerous benefits, there is a need to convey the results effectively to any viewer of the test, as an acceptance test can provide the fact that a given software can execute in a provided manner but cannot preserve this hypothesis. In this chapter, the concept of test reports in the Robot Framework will be discussed in detail, which covers understanding and customization of the generated reports through provided options, manual as well as automated changes. As the report internals are discussed in detail, report customization can be done with more confidence.

The need for reports

In order to save the events and actions that occurred during the test execution apart from what appears on the console where the results are displayed to the user, there is a need to create test reports in files as it offers numerous benefits, some of which are outlined as follows:

Quick-test run assessment

The test results can be recalled at a glance quickly if there is a standardized format that can clearly identify the success or failure of tests as well as easily determining individual test details.

Result comparison

The test results can be compared side-by-side for the same acceptance test that can be taken across different states of the same test, across different external variables, or at different times.

Individual result detailing

The test report can detail the environment and test execution steps and other data in an ordered manner that is essential to determine the success of a test execution.

Intelligent assessment

Through the use of reports and logs, it becomes a lot easier for a person to analyze the execution of a test. This is quite handy when it comes to automation tests as analyzing the causes of failure can be tedious after the test has run. The populated data can also be used to obtain necessary metrics as well infer secondary data, such as performance of tests over a period of time, and to infer other details as necessary.

Generated files

As mentioned earlier, the Robot Framework generates two HTML files that are log and report files. These are complementary to each other and while analyzing any project, you will find yourself using both of them. Apart from these files, an XML is generated by default that contains the metadata of all the output of the test results. This is helpful in in many ways that are discussed in detail in this chapter.

The log file presents the detailed execution report in a hierarchical manner based on the different test suites. It also has the test statistics, but the high level overview of tests is present in the report file. The report presents the results in multiple ways, detailed in the following sections.

Output structure

The test report contains the results of test execution under the following headlines that are explained next.

Heading

The heading is the first element of the page which contains the test name and the time when it was generated. It also displays the elapsed time since its generation.

Summary information

This contains the summary of the test, the start and end time of the test, and the total time taken in the test execution.

Test statistics

These are the number of tests that are present in the test; the various tests are grouped on the basis of their criticality, tag, and suite. By default, all the tests are critical, but you can explicitly specify whether a test is critical or not by passing `--critical` or `--noncritical` followed by the test name in the pybot/jybot command. Tags can be set/unset in tests through the use of **Set Tags/Remove Tags** keywords in test cases. Additionally, this can be specified in suite setup that tags all the test cases in that suite file.

Test details

Test details are only present in test reports and contain the same information which is present above it in test statistics; however, they provide a more concise view as the different statistics are present in tabular manner. Beneath this column is empty space but as soon as you click any test suite above, a detailed table containing various properties associated with that suite and its children appear and the test details display the information pertaining to the suite.

Test execution log

This is only present in the log file and contains all the logs generated from tests. To see the test suite hierarchy, click on the expand all button to see all the test suite hierarchies present in your tests. It contains the location of suite source files and folders, and information down to the level of keywords present within the tests.

Test coloring information

In any xUnit test result, red denotes failure and green denotes success. This coloring has also led to the popular TDD mantra of "Red, Green, Refactor" in unit tests, which denotes the order of development as first the tests are created with an intention to naturally fail followed by writing code in such a manner that the tests pass and finally refactoring over existing code can be made in such a manner that nothing is broken.

The following screenshot demonstrates a test application passing entirely as the green color background is clearly visible:

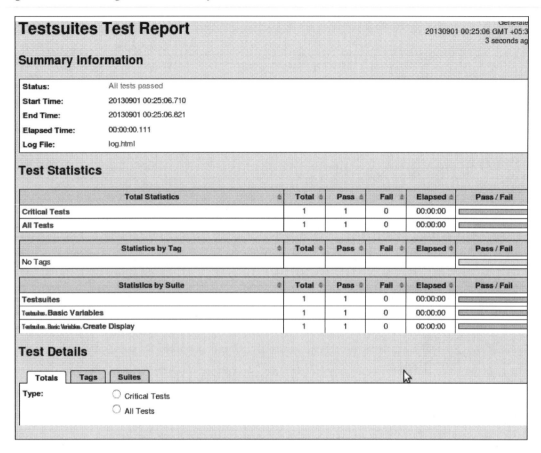

Similarly, the failure of the test suite can also be reflected through the background color. Note that, even if a single test case fails, the entire report will have the color of failure and the end user can easily take note, as shown in the following screenshot:

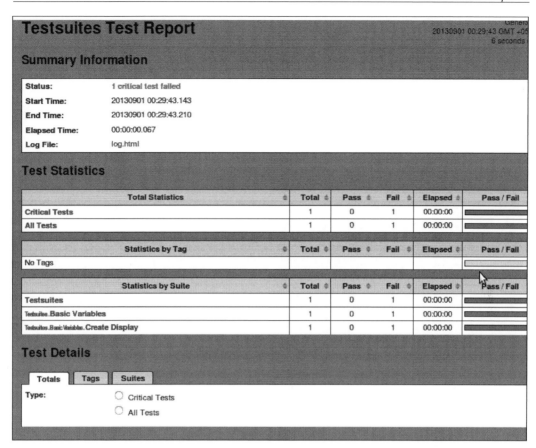

This convention is also followed in the Robot Framework as is evident from the report background color as well as the colors used in the executed tests inside the log file.

Separating files

The generated reports are generally overwritten on every execution. However, this can be made unique for every run by providing a unique name that can be provided by naming the files with a timestamp. In order to do this, the pybot/jybot/ipybot commands can be supplied with arguments that insert a timestamp along with the file name, which ensures uniqueness of the file names and ensures that no file overwrite takes place. To do this, there is a need to add the --timestampoutputs argument to these commands. This inserts the timestamp in the format, YYYYMMDD-hhmmss between the name and extension of the generated report file.

For instance, this can be used to specify the timestamped files:

```
pybot --timestampoutputs -o metadata -l log -r report testsuites
```

Making changes in outputs

Certain customizations in the generated report and log file can be made that can be used out of box in the Robot Framework. This can be helpful in setting up the test reports according to requirements without changing the report structure as well as without affecting the codebase in any manner.

Customizing the report title

The `--logtitle` and `--reporttitle` arguments can be used before the log file and report file names respectively to set their customized titles; otherwise, the defaults of the Test Log or Test Report are used wherever necessary.

 While using custom names through arguments, underscores are converted into spaces just like the test suite file and folder names.

In order to not allow files to have the standard `<root test suite> Test Report/ Log` headline, these options can be used as follows:

```
pybot --logtitle info_log -l log --reporttitle Tests_at_a_glance -r
report testsuites
```

Background color customization

The color scheme used in reports does not need to be changed as it confirms the color used in the xUnit configuration and used in most of the other tests/testing tools. However, there may some cases where this might not be as good as other alternatives for example, a color-blind person may have trouble differentiating between the default colors; this could contrast with the colors used in branding, and so on. To specify the colors, `--reportbackground successcolor:failurecolor` option is provided where the color names can be provided as is, such as red, blue, yellow, or by providing the color hex codes like #05AE04.

Changing how much is logged

The logging done in the tests can also be customized, which can help in allowing various elements and information types within the test logs. Various log levels can be assigned that allow the message to be printed under various scenarios. Some messages, however, are only issued by the Robot Framework itself, such as FAIL, which happens only when some test keyword is missing. Other messages such as Warn, Info, Debug, and Trace can also be used in problems of varying importance, which is similar to how most popular logging frameworks operate.

Also, logging can be customized by using logging APIs in Python programs where both the `robot.api.logger` as well as standard Python logging can be used.

The `--loglevel` argument is used to specify various log levels for the generated log file. If this is done at a level below info, then a dropdown appears below the report link in the log file, as shown in the following image:

Changing the report format

At times, there is a need to make slight changes in the generated reports, which can be done either by customizing a CSS for the output files or making changes in the downloaded source code and rebuilding a custom installation of the framework. In this section, both these strategies of customization are discussed.

If the log file is opened in a text editor, it will display the internally used CSS that is inline to the file. Similarly, the report also contains jQuery embedded inline. By doing this, the file can be used without any dependency over an external file or website, and the report works over any modern browser.

These files can be freely used as the user requires but the only thing to remember is that, if the reports are not generated uniquely, then the subsequent executions of the Robot Framework will override the report/log file.

To do the customization, let's use a previously generated report, where the test is already completed. As this report has already been generated, it cannot be customized. So after loading up the report in the text editor, jump to line number 1247 that contains the JavaScript function which adds the content shown at the top right of the page as shown:

```
function addHeader() {
....
                '<div id="top-right-header">' +
                  '<div id="report-or-log-link"><a href="#"></a></div>' +
                '</div>', {
            generated: window.output.generatedTimestamp,
....
```

This function loads up the time elapsed and the link to the other (log/report) file. Here, another div can be appended right after the `report-or-log-link` div that contains an image that will serve as our icon. The changed div structure within the same function therefore becomes:

```
  . . .
                '<div id="top-right-header">' +
                  '<div id="report-or-log-link"><a href="#"></a></div>' +
                  '<div id="my_custom_image"><img src="../Pictures/github-
icon.jpg" /></div>'+
                '</div>', {
            generated: window.output.generatedTimestamp,
....
```

This code will be responsible for the presence of an icon in the report. However, as this is an external image, its path must resolve correctly to the report. So, a web-based image URL can also be used if the report is to be sent between different computers or bundled together with the reports if they are also to be used offline.

Similarly, if the color of the report needs to be changed right before sending this report to the manager or stakeholder and that person prefers a specific color, then the report can be further tweaked. In line 1472, there is a JavaScript function that sets up the report color:

```
function setBackground(topsuite) {
    var color;
    if (topsuite.criticalFailed)
        color = window.settings.background.fail;
    else if (topsuite.totalFailed)
        color = window.settings.background.nonCriticalFail;
    else
        color = window.settings.background.pass;
```

```
        $('body').css('background-color', color);
    }
```

Before changing this function with hardcoded values, the colors used can be manipulated. So, this function can be used to simply set the background color to white by performing the following changes to this function:

```
    function setBackground(topsuite) {
        var color = 'White';
        $('body').css('background-color', color);
    }
```

After the previous two changes, only a page refresh is needed in order to view the changes which include the presence of an icon below the log link as well as changing the background to white.

This is quite handy while quickly adjusting the generated reports but as this process is manual, changing reports like this becomes a chore, especially if the reports are large in number or are frequently overwritten.

To solve this limitation, a custom built the Robot Framework can be used. Assuming you have access to the entire Robot Framework repository, the files present in the `src/robot/htmldata` folder can be manipulated to send any customized changes into the framework itself; after installing the Robot Framework, such changes become permanent and apply over each and every report generated from the Robot Framework.

Creating derived reports

Apart from the log and report files, an XML file is also generated as an output from each execution of the test and at times there may be a need to use these files as a basis for further analysis of tests, such as a time analysis over a piece of software. The XML file can be parsed and analyzed as per the custom requirements. In Python, processing XML is quite easy with the built in **elementtree** library and the different XML elements can be traversed as a tree and different operations can be performed over them.

Recreating reports

As mentioned earlier, the Robot Framework provides a tool to recreate test output files from the generated metadata through the use of the **rebot** tool. This tool supports all the arguments of the `pybot` command as mentioned in *Chapter 1, Getting Started with the Robot Framework* and uses only the XML file generated as an output. This is handy if the other files are not present or while storing a huge collection of test results in only the XML format. However, the most important feature of rebot lies in combining multiple XML files into a single test, which is handy if you have run the same acceptance test in different environments and want to present the results in a single file.

Suppose you have test results from different states in files such as state0.xml, state1.xml, state2.xml, and so on in your folder, then you can simply recreate a single test result with a custom named top level test suite by using:

```
rebot --name Country_Results state/*.xml
```

Viewing differences

Sometimes, you have multiple test results and want to compare the differences between themselves. To do this, a diff tool known as **robotdiff** provides comparison between test cases. This is present under the `tools/robotdiff` folder in the robotframework source. To generate the comparison, do the following:

```
python robotdiff.py output1.xml output2.xml output-n.xml
```

The default generated report is `robotdiff.html` in the user home folder and the result is titled "Test Run Diff Report" with each test name obtained from the XML file names.

Further result usage

As the generated metadata result file is in xUnit-compatible XML format, it can be used as an input for external tools that understand this format. One such example is the Jenkins plugin (`https://wiki.jenkins-ci.org/display/JENKINS/Robot+Framework+Plugin`) that supports statistics generation based on these files.

Summary

This chapter covered the output customization of the generated contents from test execution as the data and results arising out of tests can be re-used and re-analyzed. The different files and their formats used in the test outputs are detailed in order to proceed with their modification. Different methods of modifying individual reports, as well as report generation itself to suit an organization's demands, are explained. Further pointers on how to modify the framework and use programs to generate custom reports is also mentioned, along with report generation and usage of test reports.

Index

Thank you for buying
Robot Framework Test Automation

About Packt Publishing

Packt, pronounced 'packed', published its first book "*Mastering phpMyAdmin for Effective MySQL Management*" in April 2004 and subsequently continued to specialize in publishing highly focused books on specific technologies and solutions.

Our books and publications share the experiences of your fellow IT professionals in adapting and customizing today's systems, applications, and frameworks. Our solution based books give you the knowledge and power to customize the software and technologies you're using to get the job done. Packt books are more specific and less general than the IT books you have seen in the past. Our unique business model allows us to bring you more focused information, giving you more of what you need to know, and less of what you don't.

Packt is a modern, yet unique publishing company, which focuses on producing quality, cutting-edge books for communities of developers, administrators, and newbies alike. For more information, please visit our website: www.packtpub.com.

About Packt Open Source

In 2010, Packt launched two new brands, Packt Open Source and Packt Enterprise, in order to continue its focus on specialization. This book is part of the Packt Open Source brand, home to books published on software built around Open Source licences, and offering information to anybody from advanced developers to budding web designers. The Open Source brand also runs Packt's Open Source Royalty Scheme, by which Packt gives a royalty to each Open Source project about whose software a book is sold.

Writing for Packt

We welcome all inquiries from people who are interested in authoring. Book proposals should be sent to author@packtpub.com. If your book idea is still at an early stage and you would like to discuss it first before writing a formal book proposal, contact us; one of our commissioning editors will get in touch with you.

We're not just looking for published authors; if you have strong technical skills but no writing experience, our experienced editors can help you develop a writing career, or simply get some additional reward for your expertise.

Sikuli Test Automation

ISBN: 978-1-78216-787-7   Paperback: 54 pages

Discover automated application testing techniques for anything that is visible on the computer screen

1. Learn something new in an Instant! A short, fast, focused guide delivering immediate results

2. Write simple tests using the Sikuli IDE

3. Construct a framework for running your tests and reporting results

Selenium Testing Tools Cookbook

ISBN: 978-1-84951-574-0   Paperback: 326 pages

Over 90 recipes to build, maintain, and improve test automation with Selenium WebDriver

1. Learn to leverage the power of Selenium WebDriver with simple examples that illustrate real world problems and their workarounds

2. Each sample demonstrates key concepts allowing you to advance your knowledge of Selenium WebDriver in a practical and incremental way

3. Explains testing of mobile web applications with Selenium Drivers for platforms such as iOS and Android

Please check **www.PacktPub.com** for information on our titles

Chef Infrastructure Automation Cookbook

ISBN: 978-1-84951-922-9   Paperback: 276 pages

Over 80 delicious recipes to automate your cloud and server infrastructure with Chef

1. Configure, deploy, and scale your applications

2. Automate error prone and tedious manual tasks

3. Manage your servers on-site or in the cloud

4. Solve real world automation challenges with task-based recipes

Testing with QUnit

ISBN: 978-1-78328-217-3   Paperback: 64 pages

Employ QUnit to increase your efficiency when testing JavaScript code

1. Learn something new in an Instant! A short, fast, focused guide delivering immediate results

2. Learn about cross-browser testing with QUnit

3. Learn how to use popular QUnit plugins and develop your own plugins

4. Hands-on examples on all the essential QUnit methods

Please check **www.PacktPub.com** for information on our titles

07517888574

5355819R00056

Printed in Great Britain
by Amazon.co.uk, Ltd.,
Marston Gate.